BEYOND
BIBLICAL INTEGRATION

IMMERSING YOU AND YOUR STUDENTS
IN A BIBLICAL WORLDVIEW

ROGER C. S. ERDVIG

Erdvig wastes no time making clear his intention to give readers a wake-up punch in the nose! He rightly charges most of us in Christian schooling (K–12 and seminary) with not practicing what we claim or promise on our websites. Some of us don't even know what the phrase "biblical worldview" means. Many of us are stuck on the 1950s catchphrase "integration of faith and learning"—which we also haven't been implementing. Erdvig offers to use cattle prods to goad us into realization, repentance, and redemption as school leaders and classroom teachers. For all of us, such redemption includes a fuller knowledge and understanding of God's wisdom and truth as found in the close reading of Scripture, followed by obedient action.

— **Dr. D. Bruce Lockerbie**,
Chairman/CEO, PAIDEIA, Inc.

There has long been a need for this book. While there are a lot of great books on the importance of biblical worldview, most lack practical strategies for living it out. This book offers both. With experience and wisdom, Roger Erdvig lays out a vision and practical strategy for creating Christian schools immersed in worldview. *Beyond Biblical Integration* is a book every Christian educator and administrator needs to read, study, and implement.

— **Dr. Sean McDowell**,
Biola University Professor, Speaker, Author

When Christian educators believe the perspective explained in these pages, act on their new understandings, and work with their colleagues, they will secure their students' faith into their young adult years and beyond. Erdvig's ideas will challenge you and compel you to action. He is clear and practical, so you will not be overwhelmed. The way he writes about the dominant worldview of public schools caused me to gasp out loud and read several paragraphs more than once. He's right! I've been involved in Christian education for thirty-five years, and I've been concerned we weren't making the kind of difference we should be making. Erdvig teaches us what must change and how to do it. I've never read a more encouraging book for Christian educators.

— **Dr. Kathy Koch**,
Founder/President of Celebrate Kids, Inc.,
cofounder, Ignite the Family, and the author of
8 Great Smarts and *Five to Thrive*

This is the perfect book for any Christian teacher who wants to take their classroom to the next level. It's practical, insightful, and full of helpful resources. I particularly enjoyed some of the actionable classroom discussion practices. I will be using those!

— **David Eaton**,
President & Co-founder, Axis

Beyond Biblical Integration explains the why and how of biblical worldview immersion in the Christian school setting, with a strong philosophical foundation and abundant practical application. Erdvig outlines the need for a biblical worldview in a compelling manner and challenges us to create a school culture where such a worldview can flourish.

— **Steve Whitaker**,
Head of School, The First Academy (Orlando, FL)

Dr. Roger Erdvig presents a compelling argument for going beyond the teaching of a biblical worldview within our Christian schools to pursuing a complete Christian worldview *immersion* on our campuses. He offers practical steps to help educators develop, teach, and assess their progress in utilizing the Bible as a framework for all of reality. Most important, Erdvig inspires us to confidently live the gospel at our schools with joy. I plan to give a copy of this book to every member of my faculty.

— **Julie Ambler**,
Head of School, The Woodlands Christian Academy
(The Woodlands, TX)

Dr. Roger Erdvig is both an author and alchemist who, over the span of just a couple hundred pages, transforms the trappings of a traditional Christian classroom into a golden road towards true biblical worldview immersion. A quick warning for those readers undone by rapid rides and quick corners: Erdvig will help Christian school students, teachers, parents, administrators, and board members accelerate very quickly and efficiently toward actual fulfillment of the mission statements that we have boldly emblazoned across our promotional materials, websites, and social media! You will not escape the first chapter without being equipped to see your students enjoy true biblical worldview formation.

— **Geoff Brown**,
Superintendent, Northwest Christian School (Phoenix, AZ)

Beyond Biblical Integration is an excellent, practical resource that every Christian school should make required reading for each faculty and staff member. I will be recommending it to all the schools and Christian educators we work with at RenewaNation.

— **Jeff Keaton**,
President & CEO, RenewaNation

Erdvig presents us with practical steps toward creating authentic, immersive learning environments that support students in their biblical worldview development. With an understanding that student engagement is key in supporting meaningful learning, he presents helpful tips for creating effective schools and classrooms.

— **Dr. William Himmele**,
Professor of Education, Millersville University (PA),
Co-author of *Total Participation Techniques*

The classroom of today is the public policy of tomorrow. If our goal is to educate our children in a way that inoculates them against deceptive narratives and prepares them to influence and thrive in this culture, then we have to educate with the end in view. Dr. Erdvig identifies, with remarkable clarity, the challenges and the fundamental principles for every Christian parent and educator. This book meets a tremendous need and may very well be the catalyst for a paradigm shift in Christian education.

— **Nicole Theis**,
President, Delaware Family Policy Council

In an age when many of the world's cultural landscapes are being immersed in a life-destroying tsunami of secularism, Roger Erdvig's book is, indeed, timely. Dr. Erdvig proposes that in order for Christian schools to fulfill their role in advancing the Kingdom of God (while being surrounded by the *intensely unfriendly climate in which they operate*), they must begin to comprehend, create, and operate within environments *immersed* in the life-giving biblical worldview.

— **John Hay**,
Author, *Building on the Rock* curriculum

BEYOND
BIBLICAL INTEGRATION
IMMERSING YOU AND YOUR STUDENTS
IN A BIBLICAL WORLDVIEW

BEYOND BIBLICAL INTEGRATION

ISBN-13: 978-1-7330256-5-2
ISBN-10: 1-7330256-5-0
LCCN: 2020933723

Published by Summit Ministries
PO Box 207
Manitou Springs, CO 80829
www.summit.org

Second printing 2021
Printed in the United States of America

TABLE OF CONTENTS

Foreword xi
Prologue xiii

PART I: UNDERSTANDING BIBLICAL WORLDVIEW IMMERSION 1

1. Perspectives on a Biblical Worldview 3
2. Systems of Immersion 19
3. Fundamentals of a Worldview 33
4. The Center Point 47
5. How a Biblical Worldview Takes Shape 65
6. Developing Your Own Worldview 81
7. Committing to Meaningful Processing 93

PART 2: CREATING A BIBLICAL WORLDVIEW IMMERSIVE ENVIRONMENT 107

8. Shaping the Heart's Desires 117
9. Cultivating Experiences within Your *Pedagogium* 139
10. Embracing the Chaos of Engaged Learning 161
11. Teaching from a Biblical Worldview 181
12. Leading the Biblical Worldview Revolution 205

Epilogue 229
Bibliography 233
Recommended Resources 237
Endnotes 243

FOREWORD

For years the Christian education community has used the term "biblical worldview integration" to describe efforts to teach every subject from a biblical perspective.

It's time to retire that phrase.

Why? Because if the Bible is God's special revelation for everyone, everywhere, all the time, then it isn't something we integrate into whatever else we're doing. It's something we immerse ourselves in; any other truth rises out of it. God's Word isn't a partial truth that dovetails with other, "not-from-God" truths. God's Word is true truth.

Here's a new way to phrase the mission of Christian education: biblical worldview immersion.

Something exciting happens when we immerse ourselves in a biblical worldview. We realize that deep, biblical thinking is possible in every subject. We find that we can have the mind of Christ. So can our students. It will change all of us.

In the past, Christians transformed science, education, the arts, healthcare, human rights, and more. It is time for a new era of innovation—and innovation starts with immersion.

As Dr. Roger Erdvig shows in this thought-provoking work, the difference between integration and immersion is not just semantic. The Bible is not an add-on to things that are known otherwise. It's not a way to widen the keyhole of truth to get a slightly better perspective on reality. Rather, in the Bible, God throws the door of reality wide open, enabling us to understand him, the world, and our relationship to him and the world.

In the Bible, the Creator and Redeemer God reveals the shape and tempo of his nature in a way that eludes those who look only to the material world for knowledge. Matter is not all that matters.

The power of biblical worldview immersion is really why Summit Ministries exists. Our mission is to equip and support rising generations to embrace God's truth and champion a biblical worldview. I envision a day when our students will be leading pastors and missionaries, but also leading athletes, scientists, medical caregivers, politicians, diplomats, architects, painters, musicians, tradespeople, writers, teachers, media personalities, designers, manufacturers, shopkeepers…you get the idea.

So, from now on, I'm going to make it a point to stop talking about "biblical worldview integration" and start emphasizing "biblical worldview immersion."

I'm taking this step largely because I've known and worked with Dr. Erdvig for a decade and a half. He lives in the world of Christian education—with its tight budgets and strained schedules—and he knows that you don't need "one more thing" to do. That's why Dr. Erdvig approaches biblical worldview immersion as a friend and guide. He won't think for you, but he will think alongside you.

Can you tell I'm excited about this book? I hope you soon will be, too.

Jeff Myers, Ph.D., President
Summit Ministries

PROLOGUE

Tucked away in Hebrew Wisdom Literature is a unique metaphor for how our words function, specifically our words as teachers or writers. In Ecclesiastes 12:11, we're told, "The words of the wise are like goads, and like nails firmly fixed are the collected sayings." Goads and nails—they both have sharp points, but they are used for different purposes.

A goad is a tool of animal husbandry used to prod livestock into moving ahead. Getting nudged with a goad hurts. But sometimes that's what a farm animal needs in order to be persuaded to get moving. Nails serve a different purpose. They're used to fasten one piece of wood to another. Goads are about movement; nails are about permanence. The words of this book are about both.

We need to be more committed than ever to raising up great Christian young people who will advance the kingdom of God. This means firming up our understanding of our mission. This is where we need some nails. However, we also need to be prodded to think in new ways about how to accomplish our mission. This is where we need to feel the goads.

All of us in Christian educational leadership realize the intensely unfriendly climate in which we are now operating. From pre-K–12 schools all the way up to the university level, we are asking some hard questions about our future. Gone are the days that marked my own elementary years in a Christian school on Long Island. From the early 1970s to the mid-1980s, the growth of the Christian school movement continued to peak. I joke that you could hang a shingle on your church door identifying it as a Christian school, and you'd have plenty of families enrolling their kids. Since then, however, precipitous downward trends in Christian school enrollment suggest we need to take stock of what we're doing and do some things differently.

The distinguishing mark of a Christian school should be *an education that immerses students in a biblical worldview*. In the pages that follow, I'll offer both goads and nails related to this goal. Christian schools must do a better job of providing an immersive biblical worldview experience for our students if we are to remain faithful to our mission. As you read, you may think at times, "Yes, our school is already doing that!" That would be analogous to my words being nails. At other times, you may think, "Ouch! We're not doing that, and we really need to." This would be an example of a goad. I trust you'll find plenty of both as you read.

I'm not saying that if we do *x*, *y*, and *z*, our enrollment trends will dramatically reverse themselves. But if we are going to remain true to the vision of being distinctively Christian centers of teaching and learning, we have no choice. We must evaluate if and how we're creating and sustaining learning environments that are saturated with a biblical worldview.

If you're a Christian schoolteacher, I'm writing to you with an enormous level of respect and admiration. You are the heroes of successful Christian schooling. This includes everyone from the teachers who helped shape my worldview back in Huntington Christian School to the teachers whom I serve daily as head of a school.

If you're a Christian school administrator, I'm writing to you as head of a school myself. I have a deep understanding of the challenges and opportunities you face every day. My hope is that you will find great success in fulfilling your school's mission. Hopefully this book will provide a practical map for assessing and improving what you do.

I pray that my words will help us shape our schools to raise up and deploy exceptional Christian young people into the world. In our lifetime, this mission has never been more necessary or more challenging.

PART I

UNDERSTANDING
BIBLICAL WORLDVIEW
IMMERSION

CHAPTER I

PERSPECTIVES ON A BIBLICAL WORLDVIEW

THE DUNNING-KRUGER EFFECT

Have you ever noticed that people sometimes think they're much better at something than they really are? In a 1964 episode of *The Andy Griffith Show*, Deputy Barney Fife joins the Mayberry Community Choir. He eagerly auditions for a tenor solo. Since there are slim pickings for tenor soloists among the two thousand residents of Mayberry, the choir director reluctantly gives Barney the part. Everyone quickly realizes that Barney doesn't have a good enough voice—everyone, of course, except Barney. In his own perception, he's a budding virtuoso. This solo just may be his ticket to an exciting future on the stage.

We laugh at Barney and his exaggerated sense of abilities. But in real life, people sometimes really do think they are better at something than they are. This is not just the stuff of TV sitcoms.

Psychological researchers David Dunning and Justin Kruger (2000) studied this phenomenon. They developed an explanation for why people overestimate their abilities. Their explanatory model (called the Dunning-Kruger Effect) suggests that people do so because they lack *accurate self-awareness*. For some reason, like Barney, who couldn't hear what he really sounded like, people just don't always see themselves accurately.

We've all known someone who thinks more highly of himself than he ought. And we've likely entertained exaggerated assessments of ourselves as well. It seems this is part of life as human beings. We're in a constant process of becoming more self-aware. It may be okay to give Uncle Ted a pass at the Thanksgiving table when he expounds on topics he doesn't really understand. However, the stakes get a bit higher when we experience an institutional Dunning-Kruger Effect.

Christian schools aren't immune to experiencing this phenomenon. It can be hard for us to maintain accurate organizational self-awareness. When we don't see ourselves clearly, though, we can develop the unfortunate habit of overpromising and underdelivering.

Here's how this plays out. The leaders in a Christian school believe their school is proficient in certain aspects of education. So they understandably want to tell everyone how good they are in those areas. Statements of their self-perceived proficiency show up in mission statements, expected student outcomes, marketing pieces, social media posts, and so on. Implicit in these statements

is a promise that students and families will actually be the bene-
ficiaries of that proficiency. But what if the school's perception of
itself isn't accurate and the school ends up promising things it's
not able to deliver? This can be a significant breech of institutional
integrity. Unfortunately, Christian
schools unwittingly fall into the
Dunning-Kruger Effect, truly be-
lieving they're doing better at some
things than they really are.

> We tend to overpromise
> and underdeliver on
> what students will
> experience in our
> classrooms and hallways
> and what they'll be like
> when they graduate.

I've repeatedly seen this
problem in one very important
area: biblical worldview. We tend
to overpromise and underdeliver
on what students will experience in our classrooms and hallways
and what they'll be like when they graduate. Avoiding this situation
is possible, but it will take serious work and heavy doses of institutional and individual self-awareness. We in the Christian school
movement make bold promises on our websites and at our open
house events. But not enough effort and time are given to assessing
how we're really doing when it comes to delivering on those promises. As a result, we lose a sense of accurate self-awareness.

THE PROMISE OF A BIBLICAL WORLDVIEW

I'm sure you've heard the promises Christian schools make to the
families they teach. You may even have said these words yourself:
"We teach from a biblical worldview perspective"; "If your children
attend our school, they will graduate with a strong biblical worldview." I believe the goals behind these promises are central to why
we exist. But I'm not sure we've thought deeply enough about what

they mean and how they should impact every element of our students' experience.

Think about the implications of our promises. They suggest we are experts in biblical worldview (in addition to being experts in teaching and in our subject areas). We imply that we know how to nurture a strong biblical worldview in our students. But are these promises reasonable? Are we claiming we're really good at something, when in reality we are still just novices? Are we like Barney Fife, singing our hearts out while not realizing we're failing to carry the choir?

The modern discussion about worldview has its roots in the works of Francis Schaeffer, Charles Colson, Nancy Pearcy, David Naugle, James Sire, David Noebel, and many others. The concept of worldview predates these folks by almost two centuries. However, they're the ones who ushered worldview thinking from the philosopher's domain into the mainstream of evangelical Christianity over the last fifty years. Thanks to the accessible treatment of worldview concepts from these writers, the word *worldview* is now commonplace. It's readily available in books, curricula, camps, and conferences.

Along with this explosion of attention and resources has come a corollary and logical phenomenon—the recognition of the centrality of a biblical worldview in Christian education. You'd be hard-pressed to find any Christian school or university in North America that doesn't include the idea of a biblical worldview in its mission, vision, or core values. Do a quick internet search of their mission statements, and you'll find evidence that a biblical worldview is firmly ensconced in the canon of Christian education must-haves.

What you'll likely find are statements that mirror the promises I mentioned earlier ("We teach from a biblical worldview perspective" and "Our graduates have a strong biblical worldview"). Both of these promises are important. It wouldn't take much to convince you that teaching from a biblical worldview and producing graduates who have a biblical worldview should be the hallmarks of Christian schools. In the anti-Christian, anti-truth era in which we exist, I can't think of anything else more worthy to be *the* distinctives for Christian schools. But my experience in pre-K–12 Christian schools and Christian higher education leads me to an unhappy conclusion: *we have a long way to go in delivering on these promises.* And I don't mean that we know the pathway to take and are just not very far along on the journey. I mean that we don't even have the pathway well laid out.

Let me explain.

The promise that we offer an education based on a biblical worldview suggests we have put enormous effort into making sure this is indeed true. If you ask the average Christian schoolteacher about this, however, you may be surprised at his or her answer.

I did a workshop on biblical worldview for a prominent, established Christian school long after the biblical worldview movement was well established. One guy came up to me and asked, "You keep talking about something called *worldview.* What is that?" At the time, this school was like other schools, promising an education based on a biblical worldview and graduates who leave school with a strong biblical worldview. Yet one of their experienced teachers wasn't even familiar with the term.

Like this man, many of our highly qualified and skilled Christian schoolteachers don't deeply understand a biblical worldview and how it should shape what they do in the classroom. Yet they are tasked with immersing all they do in a biblical worldview and effectively inculcating that worldview in their students.

As head of two Christian schools, I have hired dozens of teachers. When I bring up the concept of teaching from a biblical worldview perspective in interviews, I'm mostly met with an uneasy look of bewilderment. That look says, "I should know what you're talking about and that it's really important if I want to get this job. But I really have no idea." As a result, I often break one of the cardinal rules of interviewing by doing too much of the talking. I explain what a worldview is and how a biblical worldview should shape teaching and learning. The responses I hear include things like "I never thought of that!" or "Wow! I'd love to learn how to teach that way."

But as my earlier story shows, the lack of understanding is not limited to the novices. Many veteran teachers are equally unfamiliar with the concept of worldview and how it shapes the teaching and learning process. I've sent many veteran teachers to biblical worldview conferences. They invariably come back with a profound realization that their approach to teaching and to their subject matter has been deconstructed and is in serious need of rebuilding. This is a great awakening. But my concern is that *these are the ones upon whom we've been depending to deliver a biblical worldview-saturated learning experience for our students.*

Across the Christian school movement, I find similar phenomena, suggesting we're not as good at this biblical worldview thing as we think we are. Don't get me wrong—I love Christian schoolteachers. (I'm married to one!) I have tremendous respect for their expertise and work ethic as educators and as wonderful

Christians. But in our fervor to generate compelling mission statements and formulate lists of attractive student outcomes, we may have neglected the most important keys to success. We need to make sure our teachers (and school leaders) have a deep, personal commitment to a thoroughly biblical worldview and how that worldview can be nurtured in students.

In addition, we need to align our teaching practices with our worldview. While this may seem obvious, research suggests that many teachers do not give much thought to how their beliefs should impact how they teach.[1]

> In our fervor to generate compelling mission statements and formulate lists of attractive student outcomes, we may have neglected the most important keys to success.

INTEGRATION IS NOT ENOUGH

My purpose is to help Christian schoolteachers and administrators think more deeply and tactically about the promises we make. We can do so by approaching our promises relating to biblical worldview with a reality I call *biblical worldview immersion*. This is not to be confused with biblical *integration*, a worthy subject about which many have written and taught.

Biblical integration is achieved when academic content is seamlessly wed to biblical content. It helps us understand what God says through the Bible, his creation, and his dealings with mankind. This applies to every academic topic and what each topic can tell us about God. Integration is certainly an important part of biblical worldview immersion, but there's much more to it. Worldview, as we shall see in later chapters, is much more than cognitive content or truth propositions. We sell worldview short when we think about it in terms of transferring cognitive knowledge alone. This is one of the weaknesses of many Christian school resources devoted to biblical worldview. It's as though we think that if we just explore the truth claims[2] of a biblical worldview with our students, they'll develop a biblical worldview. But that's not enough.

WHAT IS A BIBLICAL WORLDVIEW?

Our approach to perceiving, interpreting, and living in the world around us includes our desires, our behaviors, and the propositions we hold to be true. Ideally, all three of these (also described as inclinations, actions, and truth claims) are consistent and cohesive. They make up our worldview and combine to form a pattern of ideas, beliefs, convictions, and habits. We use these to make sense of God, the world, and our relationship to God and the world (Myers and Noebel, 2015). So a person with a biblical worldview is one who thinks, desires, and acts in ways that are consistent with God's thoughts, desires, and actions as revealed through Scripture.

Though truth claims are not the sum total of a person's worldview, they do form its foundation. And for a well-formed biblical worldview, these truth claims are not random, unrelated ideas. Together, they make up an integrated narrative framework that accurately describes the way things are. A narrative framework is essentially a story of the world that provides a context for understanding why things happen the way they do and how we should respond to what happens. The narrative framework for a biblical worldview can be summarized in four key words. They are chronological in nature and provide meaning for all our experiences: *Creation, Fall, Redemption,* and *Restoration.*

Creation refers to God's original design, structure, and function of the cosmos. *Fall* represents all that has catastrophically and progressively gone wrong with creation after Adam and Eve chose to throw off God's authority in favor of their own self-rule. *Redemption* is the work of Christ (into which he invites us) in restoring all things to their proper prefall position, purpose, and possibilities. *Restoration* is the future and final fix for the entire universe, where all things will once again be brought into proper alignment with Christ.

To make these concepts more memorable, I like to substitute four simpler words which mean the same things: *ought, is, can,* and *will.* The original creation is the way things *ought* to be. The fall has given us the new reality that *is.* Redemption is the promise and power to transform things into what they *can* be. And at the final restoration, all things *will* be made right.

The biblical worldview is a way of thinking, desiring, and acting consistently within this four-word framework for human experience. It's a way of being in which we as human beings participate in God's grand plan to transform parts of what *is* to the way things *can* be, in anticipation of when all things *will* be as they *ought* to be. An education rooted in this reality will be immersed in these concepts at every turn and in every subject area and classroom. But this is just the starting point.

BEGINNING WITH THE END IN VIEW

But beyond the day-to-day experience in school that should reflect these realities, this way of looking at a biblical worldview should also shape our endgame. The ultimate goals we have for our students are more than walking across the stage to grab their diploma and give a thumbs-up to Mom and Dad. As I said before, this is one of the areas in which I think we in the Christian school movement are overselling ourselves.

Most Christian schools I've worked with or whose websites I've visited claim to produce graduates with a strong biblical worldview. This is a huge claim—think about it. If having a biblical worldview means a person thinks, desires, and acts in concert with God's narrative, claiming that someone has a strong biblical worldview is a bold thing. It's even bolder when that person is seventeen or eighteen years old. It's hard to find church elders about whom that claim could be made! My first question when I hear (or make) such a claim is "How do I know this?" followed closely by "Is it measurable?" and "Is this more of a hunch or a hope?"

> Even if students know and can repeat the truths of a biblical worldview, it doesn't guarantee they have any inclination to live out the implications in their behavior.

The claim of producing graduates with a strong biblical worldview is often based on an assumption that we have done a decent job of teaching the truths of a biblical worldview. But even if students know and can repeat the truths of a biblical worldview, it doesn't guarantee they have any inclination to live out the implications in their behavior. All of us probably know students who can give all the right answers. But at the same time, they are making behavioral choices in direct contradiction to those answers. So we settle for students (and graduates) being able to recite proper answers, perhaps even on a worldview survey. But we don't dig any deeper to see if those students are inclined to live out the implications of those truths or if their behaviors reflect those truths. At best we have one third of the equation in hand.

Imagine if a trade school claimed to produce master electricians. But they only required their students to take a written exam on the truths of the field of electricity in order to graduate. No one would take that trade school (or their graduates) seriously if they didn't also require their students to work in the field. Students would need to live out the implications of the truths they learned in the classroom. And no one would hire them if they didn't demonstrate the ability to actually work with electricity properly. No one would accept the claim that a student fresh out of trade school could be considered a master electrician. We intuitively know the title "master electrician" would only be conferred after years of successful experience and practical tutelage with recognized master electricians.

But on a regular basis, Christian schools make the claim that they produce graduates able to represent and defend a biblical world-view in the marketplace of ideas. Really? Is that even possible without years of experience and ongoing tutelage from biblical worldview masters? Is that a claim you'd even be confident to make about yourself?

A MORE AUTHENTIC APPROACH

So what are we to do? I'm not saying we should give up hope and strike all language relating to biblical worldview from our Christian school mottoes and mission statements. Nor should we cower in despair because the work required to realign our mission statements and our actions is too great. Instead, I'm offering a straightforward set of actions and commitments for Christian schoolteachers and leaders that can nurture a more authentic approach to biblical worldview.

My approach is based on almost thirty years of experience in walking with fellow Christians as they struggle to develop a biblical worldview. I've worked with youth group members, my own five children, thousands of "adopted" children through homeschool cooperatives and Christian schools, and undergraduate and graduate students. It's also based on doctoral research I've done with exemplary Christian emerging adults who have taught me much about what it means to develop a biblical worldview.

A central premise of this book is that it's not helpful to think in terms of whether or not our students have a "strong" biblical worldview. Instead, it's more appropriate and accurate to consider whether a person has, or does not have, a *developing* biblical worldview. Here's where my research has provided for me a comprehensive way of looking at biblical worldview development.

After hundreds of hours discussing their worldviews with the emerging adults in my study, I analyzed their experiences and reflections. I discovered something deceptively simple that can easily be overlooked. And it's also at the core of how we should rethink our educational practices and goals in Christian schools. I discovered that, even for those who appear to have a strong biblical worldview, at best they have a *developing* worldview. Each one of them could demonstrate they have learned the biblical worldview answers to big questions, such as:

- "Why am I here?"
- "What is the chief aim of man?"
- "What is the meaning of human history?"
- "Can we know anything for sure?"

However, each of them also readily acknowledged that they had a long way to go in learning how to actually live out the

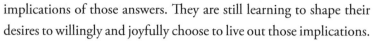

implications of those answers. They are still learning to shape their desires to willingly and joyfully choose to live out those implications.

My solution to our problem is not to give up on the idea of keeping the biblical worldview as the centerpiece of our schools. The solution is to focus on biblical worldview *development* in our teaching and goals. Doing so addresses our two challenges: how to structure the overall learning experience of our students and how to think about ultimate student outcomes.

In its simplest form, the solution is a set of specific actions and general ways of interacting with students. These actions need to be consistent with the way a person's worldview develops, particularly *after* the high school years. A comprehensive and specific birth-to-grave model for worldview development has not been articulated in the literature. So we're still limited in our understanding of this lifelong process. But we can look at what professor and researcher Sharon Parks (1981, p. 108) calls "the critical period"—the developmental stage between eighteen and twenty-three years old. If we then work backwards from that starting point, we can more authentically nurture the biblical worldview development of our youngest learners all the way through their high school years.

We'll examine ways to cultivate an environment in which students acquire the thoughts, desires, and habits they'll need to develop their worldview throughout their entire lives. Specifically, I'm suggesting our schools must be marked by the following:

1. Teachers who are actively developing their own worldview
2. Teachers who understand how a biblical worldview develops in emerging adults
3. Teachers who can create a classroom experience that fosters biblical worldview development

4. Teachers who know how a biblical worldview of reality (*ought, is, can, will*) shapes understanding of their subject area(s) and how the four key applied-worldview questions relate to their subject area

5. Leadership (from the board to the administration team) that equips and expects teachers to do all the above

MOVING BEYOND INTEGRATION

I hope you are beginning to see that the concept of biblical world-view immersion is much more than marrying Bible truths to academic content. In his book *On Christian Teaching* (2018), Professor David Smith provides historical context for shaping how we think about teaching that goes well beyond *integration* to *immersion*.

In a common mode of education in the Middle Ages, students lived with the teacher in a communal living space called a *pedagogium*.[3] In this way, the students' and teacher's entire lives would be holistically shaped by an intensely relational, practical, and immersive learning experience. But don't panic. I'm not going to suggest your twenty-two third graders move in with you. However, I suggest you consider your classroom more as a place to live and learn with your students than a place where you deliver lessons.

> Consider your classroom more as a place to live and learn with your students than a place where you deliver lessons.

If getting content across to our students is our aim, then we will continually fall short of biblical worldview immersion. Instead, we'll focus our efforts on clever ways to append what we have already planned with Bible verses and ideas. However, we can recognize that we are in the process of developing a biblical worldview of our own. We can see our classrooms as spaces in which we live for a season with our students. We can give careful attention to intentionally shaping the experience students have in relation to us and our course content. Then it will be easier to understand what it means to offer an education that is holistically based on a biblical worldview. And that will produce graduates who are well along on the journey of developing a biblical worldview.

CHAPTER 2

SYSTEMS OF
IMMERSION

In chapter 1, I introduced the idea of biblical worldview immersion and gave a general idea of the steps that can be taken to cultivate an immersive environment. Before we get into the specifics of how to cultivate such an environment, it's important to describe biblical worldview *immersion* in more detail, especially in contrast to the more popular term, biblical worldview *integration*.

HOW A MAGNET SCHOOL DOES IT . . . OR NOT

To begin, I'll tell you about a recent trip to visit a Christian teacher in a local magnet/charter school. My purpose in going was based on some assumptions I had about what the school would be like.

I'd passed this particular school many times, and every time I wondered what was going on inside. It was clearly branded as a school for the arts, even from the sign on the street and the décor on the outside of the building. I imagined art everywhere—in classrooms and hallways. I assumed the teachers were accomplished artists, instrumentalists, actors, and singers who were also qualified to teach science, math, or foreign language courses. I wondered how they might approach STEM classes from an art perspective and how the teachers would seamlessly weave artistic themes, concepts, and practical applications into every lesson. I thought about the processes for hiring, induction, and professional development, ensuring teachers would be living out the vision and mission of the school.

Unfortunately, as I sat with eager questions for my new friend, I was quickly disappointed with the reality he shared with me. In this teacher's estimation, the school was a great school when compared with other public schools. But I realized my assumptions about this magnet school were too idealistic. With wistful sighs, he told me that years ago the school was much more intentional about immersing students in the arts. Now, the school focuses more on standardized testing results in the academic disciplines. So while it still offers a great arts program when compared with other public schools, it's just a *program* rather than an immersive experience where everything in the school revolves around the arts.

As I listened to his story, I couldn't help but draw some parallels between what is going on in this magnet school and what I've experienced in Christian schools. We may have great Bible and chapel programs and even lots of Scripture injected into the classroom. But unless we've intentionally made a biblical worldview the centerpiece of all we do, we may fall into the same pattern as this magnet school. We end up promoting ourselves as providing an immersive experience (though perhaps not in those precise words), while actually delivering something far less in scope and value.

Imagine you were called upon as a consultant to help get this magnet school back on track in providing an immersive arts experience. Where would you start? It certainly would not be enough to get the teachers to merely reintegrate arts-related content into their lessons. A great start, yes. But the full solution, no. If you wanted to get significant results, it would take much more of a wholesale re-thinking and reorienting of all the school does. This would include teacher hiring, induction, development, and evaluation processes; design, arrangement, and branding of the physical space; curriculum; admissions standards; parent orientation; and so on. This list is only a portion of what would need to change in order to say the school offered a truly immersive experience in the arts.

My experience at the magnet school suggested an uncomfortable question. What kinds of educational institutions truly offer an education immersed in a particular worldview? The answer I came up with is perhaps more uncomfortable—public schools.

THE PUBLIC SCHOOL SYSTEM OF IMMERSION

The dominant worldview of the public school system in the United States is secularism, which is based on two central truth claims: (1) there is no reality outside of the material world (in other words, *no God*), and (2) religion, while perhaps helpful for an individual's private life, is actually a destructive force when applied in the public arena.

Two other worldviews are close cousins to secularism: postmodernism and Marxism. Both these worldviews have significant influence in the public school system as well. Postmodernism hypocritically posits that it's not possible to arrive at an agreement about the truth. Marxism is a view of reality that assumes all conflict in the world is a result of the rich oppressing the weak and the solution for this conflict is to empower the weak.[4] While postmodernism and Marxism influence the public school system, they both emerge from a "there is no God" perspective. So we'll consider secularism to be *the* core worldview that drives the public school system.

Looking at any American public school's approach to education, you'll find ample evidence of complete *immersion* in secularism. From the hangings on the wall, to classroom content and pedagogy, to their stated core values and their teacher preparation and professional development programs, it's all about immersing students in an environment that factors God out of the equation and keeps man's ideas and progress at the center of it all. Science, math, language arts, social studies, and French are all viewed and taught from this perspective. Textbooks for each of these disciplines are overtly written from a secularist perspective.

If you look at a public schoolteacher's lesson plans, I'm pretty sure you won't find a column labeled "Secular Integration." Teachers don't have to think long and hard about how to bring those ideas to bear on the experience of their students. It just

> From the hangings on the wall, to classroom content and pedagogy, to their stated core values and their teacher preparation and professional development programs, it's all about immersing students in an environment that factors God out of the equation and keeps man's ideas and progress at the center of it all.

comes naturally—the *entire system is designed for immersion*—from the teacher training programs in state universities to expectations for prom night.

This is why I believe that biblical worldview integration should not be our goal. Our chief educational competitor is well beyond integration, offering an authentic immersion experience in the worldview that drives the entire public school enterprise. If we want to stand out as offering a truly unique experience—like a magnet school for families that share a biblical worldview—how could we settle for anything less than complete immersion?

IMMERSION VS. INTEGRATION

At the most fundamental level, the term integration implies that the state of things before integration happens is dis-integration. If we're talking about biblical worldview integration in Christian schools, we're suggesting that the truth contained in academic subjects is separate from a biblical worldview, and that's not accurate. We may not see clearly how a biblical worldview relates to a subject area, and quite possibly may do a shabby job of explaining how a subject area looks through the lens of a biblical worldview. But it is impossible to actually dis-integrate or separate a biblical worldview from *anything*. As Abraham Kuyper is famous for saying, "There is not a square inch in the whole domain of our human existence over which Christ, who is Sovereign over all, does not cry, 'Mine!'" If we believe this to be true, then the very idea of dis-integration is nonsensical.

The problem, then, that the biblical worldview integration movement is trying to solve is actually more of a perception problem than a problem of reality. We perceive that, at some time in scholastic history, academic learning marched off into one corner, and biblical worldview sloughed off into another, and ever since then they've been detached, or dis-integrated. Now, almost like a referee in a boxing match, Christian educators are trying to bring the two back into the center of the ring, working hard to make sure they play nicely together.

The idea here is that they have to coax the two from their respective corners. They only do that coaxing a few times throughout the day, when it's time for biblical worldview integration to happen. As a result, most of the time they're involved with learning out in the middle of the ring, while biblical worldview sits quietly in the corner by itself, waiting to be called up for the game. Then frequently, periodically, or only occasionally, they summon biblical worldview to center ring to have its rightful moments in the classroom. The frequency and effectiveness with which they do this is largely dependent upon the teacher's prowess in the ring. But like I said before, this is not reflective of reality. It's a perception of reality, and the key is not merely adding a column for biblical worldview in lesson plans. Ironically, I believe that approaching biblical worldview from an integration perspective can actually work against the very issue we think we're solving.

And while we're talking about biblical worldview being pushed to the corner, does the opposite kind of dis-integration ever happen? I find that new Christian schoolteachers who have come from public school often slip into a different kind of dis-integration largely because they are so excited to be able to talk about Scripture and pray in class. (*Finally!*) I once hired a retired public school-teacher to fill a midyear vacancy. He was highly recommended by a school parent and by his pastor. He was successful in teaching some tough high school courses.

After one meeting with this guy, I knew he had a heart of gold. However, I came to discover that he spent the first fifteen minutes of each upper-level science class leading devotions and praying with and for his students. He was almost giddy, like the proverbial kid in a candy shop. On its own merits and in a different context, what he was doing was honorable. But he created one of those rare situations where academic learning was supplanted by an emphasis on isolated aspects of biblical worldview and faith development.

I've also seen this in athletic coaching in Christian schools. A coach is so excited to have a platform to disciple students that athletic training gets minimized in favor of training in godliness. Of course, training in godliness is enormously important. But I'm not sure how much it helps the team post wins on the scoreboard, especially when it's done in place of practicing plays they need in their games. In these cases, the Bible was summoned from the bench while academic learning or athletic development patiently waited for devotions to finish.

Another former public schoolteacher I once knew said that "bringing Jesus" into the classroom was the best part of working at a Christian school. She loved being able to talk about the Lord to her students, reminding them of his love and grace. But she didn't connect talking about Christ with what the students were learning in math. The two remained separate. These examples show how a different kind of dis-integration can happen.

In either scenario, the problem is that Christian schools, by their own doing (or perhaps *un*doing), have dis-integrated two things that can't be separated at all, according to Kuyper. This can't happen any more than separating the spirit from the body without actually killing the person. Sure, a person may pay more attention to the body or to the spirit at any given time, but they can't be separated and still be a living being.

Don't get me wrong. I'm not opposed to integration. Bringing a biblically informed understanding into every subject area and topic is a good thing. It just doesn't go far enough, if we're promising that we teach from a biblical worldview perspective and that we develop students who have a strong biblical worldview.

A good number of writers have tackled the concept of biblical worldview integration, offering helpful definitions and descriptions. Overman and Johnson (2003) define biblical worldview integration as "making the connections between the pieces of life and God's larger frame of reference" (p. 28). I like their definition, but it actually supports my contention that the biblical worldview integration movement only goes so far. Like others, Overman and Johnson do a good job of equipping teachers to look at the content they are teaching with an eye toward making explicit connections between that content and the truth claims of a biblical worldview. But this is only one element needed to create an immersive experience, and focusing on integration alone is not sufficient if we want to make good on our promises.

There's another problem with integration. Writers who focus on integration tend to include detailed charts and tables for integrating a biblical worldview into lesson plans and classroom activities. I find many of those templates to be prohibitively complex and unrealistic. The teachers I know do not draw up extensively detailed lesson plans and then teach from them. Instead, they plan out their week's topics and learning activities and work from a skeleton guide. In my own teaching at the university level, I plan my class sessions in advance. But much of what I do in the classroom is not outlined in specific steps on paper. With all the demands of teaching and the administrative work that goes along with it, the average Christian schoolteacher or professor doesn't have the time to develop the kind of plans that some writers suggest are essential for effective connections to biblical worldview.

So what would Christian educational institutions look like if we never relegated biblical worldview or learning to their own corners until summoned to center ring? What if learning and biblical worldview were so inextricably bound to one another that you couldn't really see where one ends and the other starts?

WHAT DOES IMMERSION LOOK LIKE?

Moses described this kind of school when he painted a vivid picture of how children in the nation of Israel should be immersed in God's words (Deuteronomy 6:7–9; 11:18–20). To the ancient Jews, these were much more than miscellaneous laws and dictates that needed to be integrated into real life. God's words formed the unseen foundation from which they were nourished and to which they were anchored—their worldview. To effectively pass on that worldview, parents (and by extension teachers) were told to teach it diligently, to talk about it all the time from morning to night, at home, on the road, and everywhere in between. They were even told to display elements of a God-saturated worldview on their hands and their heads, as well as their doorframes and gates. Literally, everywhere (and every time) children turned, they would find themselves immersed in a God-shaped worldview.

Let's imagine we are visiting a Christian school that immerses students in a biblical worldview like Moses described. What would we see and experience in that environment? Whether on the athletic field, during the chapel service, or in AP English Literature, students in a school that immerses them in biblical worldview are challenged and supported to think, desire, and act in ways that are consistent with God's truth as revealed in Scripture.

> Whether on the athletic field, during the chapel service, or in AP English Literature, students in a school that immerses them in biblical worldview are challenged and supported to think, desire, and act in ways that are consistent with God's truth as revealed in Scripture.

From the first moments on campus in the morning, students step into a unique world—one in which even the décor in the hallways serves to bring a biblical worldview to bear on every experience throughout the day. Images paired with core worldview questions and propositions are everywhere. The school's annual worldview theme features prominently in both words and pictures around campus. Bulletin boards lack the typical secular humanist mantras of "Respect others" and "Be your best self." Instead they remind students of who they belong to and what God's purpose is for their lives and the lives of all humans. Even the bulletin board outside the math department office points to the Creator and his order as revealed in mathematics.

In the mornings, quiet music is played over the school PA system—classical, jazz, worship, and Christian pop and hip-hop—selected to expose students to the multiple genres of music that can cultivate an appreciation of all kinds of aesthetic beauty. Interactions with teachers on the way to class are marked by joy. Students are expected to look for opportunities to actively respond to the four applied worldview questions (which we'll discuss later), even when walking in the hallway. The answers to these applied worldview questions aren't relegated to some point in the future when students will be serving in real jobs in the real world. Instead, students find support and encouragement to exercise their creating, cultivating, curing, and curbing responsibilities in the smallest ways around school.

This extends to the classroom as well, where service-learning projects based on these questions feature prominently. Students get into the community to apply and extend what they're learning in their courses for the benefit of others—they do real work to meet the real needs of real people. Learning in this school is not about students becoming their best self and building their own academic résumés. It is about developing skills, knowledge, and inclinations to effectively serve others for the glory of God. They learn to serve and serve to learn.

When it comes to the actual day-to-day approach to teaching, every teacher has been trained to think through the worldview implications of *how* they teach, not just *what* they teach. Of course, they've considered the content in all their classes to ensure they are teaching what is true. But teachers in this school also know that the truth needs to be deeply processed by students, not merely consumed. This processing by students is designed to help them develop their worldview and is done in the context of authentic relationships.

Teachers seamlessly weave biblical worldview truths into every topic. They ask penetrating questions that help students analyze subject-specific truth claims and explore the practical implications of those truth claims. Teachers don't shy away from controversial subjects. Students learn the arguments for naturalistic evolution alongside the truth claims of biblical creationism. In fact, healthy, vigorous debate is a central element of teaching and learning here—even to the point of requiring students to defend positions with which they don't agree in order to help them think more clearly and more biblically about issues.

All this takes place in classrooms that are physically, emotionally, and spiritually arranged to support worldview development. Just like the hallways and common areas in the school, classrooms are filled with wall hangings. They are not empty-space fillers but intentional signposts for biblical worldview themes placed on the modern counterparts to Moses's doorframes and gates.

In the moments before class begins, teachers greet students personally at the door as they arrive, knowing that truth and relationships are the two strands of the DNA of transformational learning. For elementary students, their relationship with their classroom teacher is fostered by hours together each day exploring God's created order. Teachers share their lives as much as they do their course content, each one creating an effective and compelling *pedagogium* for their students. Lesson planning is as much about designing an environment for learning as it is planning content to transmit.

> Truth and relationships are the two strands of the DNA of transformational learning.

Students are called to an appropriately high standard of behavior, based on honoring Christ and honoring one another. This standard forms the foundation for all interactions in the school, and each teacher consistently holds all students to that standard.

Every cocurricular or extracurricular activity is measured against a biblical worldview, from the soccer field to the junior high dance. Far from a prudish avoidance of fun or competition, these appealing activities are harnessed for worldview development. Coaches and adult chaperones are expected to embrace a biblical worldview and understand how such a worldview develops. Even the songs played at basketball games are chosen based on how they reflect a biblical worldview—not merely on whether they are Christian songs or not. Many Christian songs do not promote a biblical worldview, and quite a few non-Christian songs do. Rather than strict, category-based boundaries around what's in and what's out, students are led to critically examine what they consume and promote, holding on to the good and letting go of the not-so-good and the bad.

Teachers are strongly supported by school leadership as they continue to develop their own worldview. Leadership honors research-based means of effective professional development, tying all development experiences to school vision and mission, requiring teachers to be reflective practitioners, and expecting teachers to be highly collaborative. Walls between classrooms are "permeable" and teachers connect regularly to discuss what they're learning and teaching and to sharpen, encourage, and pray for one another.

School leadership has set a clear and detailed vision for what immersive teaching and learning look like. They frequently provide feedback to teachers based on that vision. Parents also understand what teaching and learning look like in this school. All prospective and new parents are oriented to the school's mission to immerse students in a biblical worldview. Throughout the year, parents are provided ample opportunities to develop their own worldview through resources and training experiences provided or sponsored by the school. The school is marked by an expansive expectation that everyone and everything is, day by day, being more and more aligned to the contours of a biblical worldview.

I hope this brief glimpse into a school that offers an immersive biblical worldview experience has prompted you to become more self-aware—that you see yourself, your classroom, and your school more accurately. Are you shaping your students' experience according to a Deuteronomy 6 immersive biblical worldview? How far can your students get on any given day before they are saturated with

> How far can your students get on any given day before they are saturated with biblical worldview truths and life-giving relationships?

biblical worldview truths and life-giving relationships? Are your students consistently led to think, desire, and act in ways that reflect who God is and his purposes for mankind?

I've asked you these questions to help whet your appetite for chapter 3. That's where we'll begin to practically pursue the kind of school and classrooms I've just described. And it starts with you— the teacher—and your worldview. After all, you can't be expected to create immersive biblical worldview experiences for your students if you're not crystal clear on what a worldview is and how closely your worldview aligns with God's.

---- CHAPTER 3 ----

FUNDAMENTALS OF A
WORLDVIEW

THE FORMATIVE YEARS

I am almost exclusively a product of Christian schooling, starting in kindergarten with Mrs. Wooten in the parsonage basement at West Hills Baptist Church on Long Island. My public-school experience includes just one semester in the New York State university system. I also count a one-day visit with a friend at his junior high school when I was in eighth grade to see for myself if the grass was greener over there. (It wasn't.) In total, I've spent twenty-four years in Christian K–12, undergraduate, graduate, and doctoral programs. However, the first twelve years of my education—from 1974 to 1986, my most formative years—did not include any overt emphasis on a biblical worldview.

This makes sense if you consider that Francis Schaeffer's seminal book *How Should We Then Live?* had only been published in 1976. He is credited with introducing the worldview concept into the evangelical mainstream. Previously, the concept of a biblical worldview had primarily been the domain of thinkers and institutions in the Calvinistic and the Christian and Dutch Reformed traditions (Naugle, 2002). But it wasn't until Charles Colson and Nancy Pearcy wrote *How Now Shall We Live?*—their 1999 work that played on Schaeffer's title—that the broader North American Evangelical community of believers and their educational institutions became conversant with worldview concepts.[5]

Of course, back in my K–12 days, I'm sure we discussed issues and ideas that would later be classified as worldview concepts. But at the time, Christians didn't see Christianity as an overarching framework for interpreting and living within the reality around us. Like most Christian kids who grew up in the 70s and 80s, my understanding of reality was disjointed, or as Schaeffer (1981) described, in "bits and pieces."

MY WORLDVIEW JOURNEY

My first exposure to the idea of worldview was in my undergraduate program in biblical studies, in which I had to take a philosophy course. One text for the course was *Contours of a Worldview*, a 1983 classic by Arthur Holmes. I'm a bit ashamed to admit that I don't remember reading it at the time. (Sorry, Dr. Brubaker!) I'll get back to this book later in my story.

My next experience with worldview didn't actually involve the word *worldview* as such. I was a young pastor in upstate New York. My senior pastor's wife gave me *The Great Dinosaur Mystery and the Bible*, by Paul S. Taylor, published in 1987. It unpacked ideas about when and how dinosaurs may have existed. I'm amazed that I never struggled with this conundrum before my mid-twenties. I find this strange, since dinosaurs were a huge part of my growing-up years.

Like any boy in America in the 1970s, I was enthralled with dinosaurs, largely fueled by a particular genre of movies, to which I was addicted. I endured weekdays in anticipation of the weekends, and I spent my Saturday mornings watching monster movies on TV. I was an expert in these films, which included the original versions of *King Kong vs. Godzilla, Mothra vs. Godzilla*, and *Mighty Joe Young*. There was a great draw to watching colossal apes and lizards smashing through hapless Asian or West Coast cities, decimating everything in their path while military units fruitlessly attempted to end the carnage. When the movies ended, I would go to a friend's house to play King Kong and Godzilla. We'd recreate entire movie sequences involving smashing towers of blocks, stepping on Matchbox cars, and fighting slow-motion battles on makeshift sets in our backyards.

At some point in my early dinosaur-fan years, my uncle gave me a book on dinosaurs that helped develop my passion, published by the Sinclair Fuel Company. (He probably got it for filling up his car.) It had detailed pictures of T. rexes, stegosaurs, and other classic dinos. It was the only "authoritative" work on dinosaurs I had ever seen, and I read it many times over. But beyond my binge-watching of monster movies and the gas-station book, I had no teaching on dinosaurs—not in my Christian school, at church, or at home. Dinosaurs existed for me in the realm of fantasy, and I had no space in my intellectual or spiritual framework for them to live.

When I read the book from my pastor's wife, for the first time a seemingly random interest became connected to a larger story of reality. It was exhilarating. While this one book certainly didn't resolve all my questions about dinosaurs, it awakened in me a desire to explore how dinosaurs and other random interests might fit into a cohesive understanding of the way things really are.

During this time, another book providentially landed in my possession. In the years prior to online book shopping, the best means to find good books involved browsing at bookstores. Even better, conferences, festivals, or fairs had book vendors. At one such event, I happened upon a book that still reverberates in my spirit today: *Redeeming the Routines: Bringing Theology to Life*, by Robert Banks.

This was one of those game-changing books for me. It unpacked a vision of living daily life immersed in the theology we say we believe. While Banks didn't use the term *worldview* in his book, he discussed all kinds of mundane topics—like sleep, work, and leisure time—from a theological perspective. He essentially connected the dots for me, showing that every single facet of life could be interpreted and lived out within the grand scope of God's vision for the way life should be. I remember devouring Banks's work, captivated by the reality that God had something to say about every facet of human experience. I began to apply what I was learning to my daily habits. I worked, slept, played, and consumed media differently. I stepped into a whole new world that was beginning to make cohesive sense to me.

> Every single facet of life could be interpreted and lived out within the grand scope of God's vision for the way life should be.

Fast forward a few years, and things really began to gel for me. However, I did not use the term *worldview* yet, and I was not effectively assembling or connecting things in a way that would resemble a conscious worldview. I just explored thoughts and ideas and behaviors in new and more intentional ways, seeking to make connections among them. That exploration was primarily driven by the books I was reading and what I was discussing with my wife and friends. But I still did not have a vision for how I could bring all these things together, nor did I possess the tools to do so.

At the time, I was leading a church planting team, and it fell to me to do most of the preaching. My preparation each week involved many hours of reflection and thought, most often through journaling. I still have my original clothbound marble journals from that time. Reading through them shows the incremental development of my understanding of worldview, punctuated by one particular sermon series for which I was preparing.

CHRISTIANITY IS A WORLDVIEW!

In a series on the Sermon on the Mount, I decided to tackle Matthew 5 through 7 over the course of several months. This required me to do some heavy reflective lifting. While on vacation with my family, I continued my studies at poolside. In the process of repeatedly going over the text, praying, writing, and thinking deeply about the practical implications of Christ's words, I stumbled upon a jarringly disruptive thought. Christianity is not merely a set of rules or propositions to obey; nor is it solely a "personal relationship with Christ." In that moment, it dawned on me that Christianity is a comprehensive framework and overarching view of reality within which I could orient my entire being and find ultimate meaning and fulfillment. (Yes, my realization was that technical sounding, but it was full of life for me.) I blurted out on the journal page, "Christianity is a worldview!" I think I surprised myself since that wasn't a word I used at that time. David Naugle suggests that conceiving Christianity as a worldview is one of the most significant developments in the last 150 years of church history (Naugle, 2002). It certainly was that kind of watershed moment for me.

I was away from home and the internet wasn't readily available yet. So I had to wait for my vacation to end to do more research on this idea. When I got home, I went straight to my college textbooks. I vaguely remembered a book that had something to do with the word *worldview*. Thankfully, Arthur Holmes's *Contours of a Worldview* was still on my shelf. I read it as fast as I could, marking it up like a person who had just found a priceless treasure. I was hooked. That time over twenty years ago sparked a much more intentional journey of assembling and formalizing my understanding of the concept of a worldview, formed by Scripture first.

In chapter 5, I'll share what my research shows about how a biblical worldview is formed. As a teaser, I'll let you know now that *we can't shape a person's worldview by transmitting information alone.* Even if we take great pains to clearly explain God's view on every possible topic, we've only done part of the work of shaping a worldview. Why is that? It's because a worldview is much more than information alone. As we'll see in the next section, a worldview certainly includes what a person knows, but it also includes what a person desires *and* how a person behaves. Before we get into these three dimensions of a worldview, let's investigate where this term originally came from and how it is used today.

ORIGINS OF THE WORD *WORLDVIEW*

The word *worldview* was first coined by the German philosopher Immanuel Kant in the late 1790s. In German, the word is *weltanschauung*. I don't recommend that you attempt to pronounce it or use it in class with your sixth graders. It's enough to know that Immanuel Kant (1790/1987) characterized a person's worldview as a super-sensible substrate. By this, he meant that all people have an unseen foundation and source for their beliefs, thoughts, and actions.

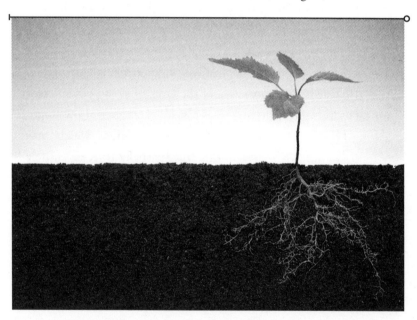

In geology, a substrate is the layer below the surface layer, unseen but exerting tremendous influence on what we can see. Think of a plant that grows in topsoil. What you perceive with your eyes is only part of the story, though rich topsoil often gets the most attention when it comes to growing healthy plants. What you can't see is the substrate. That's where plants are anchored as their roots push deep below the topsoil in a quest for stability. In addition to stability, the substrate is also the unseen source of the minerals and other nutrients needed for growth. A person's worldview functions in the same way—providing an anchor and nourishment for one's life.

Building upon Kant's ideas, many writers have given helpful explanations of the concept of worldview. My favorite comes from James Sire (2015). Faithful to the idea that a worldview is three-dimensional, Sire suggests that a worldview is "a commitment, a fundamental orientation of the heart, that can be expressed as a story or in a set of presuppositions (assumptions which may be true, partially true, or entirely false) which we hold (consciously or subconsciously, consistently or inconsistently) about the basic constitution of reality, and that provides the foundation on which we live and move and have our being" (p. 141). This explanation requires some unpacking.

> We must keep a person's desires and inclinations at the forefront when we're working to nurture his or her worldview.

1. "A Commitment, a Fundamental Orientation of the Heart"

Sire begins with the idea of a heart orientation or a commitment as the starting place for a person's worldview. According to Dallas Willard, a person's heart is the core of his or her being. It's the part of a person that makes decisions and manages his or her life (Willard, 2002). It's also the facet of our being that establishes who or what we worship or order our lives around.

The heart is the domain of desires and is the wellspring of

a person's worldview. It is easy to ignore the heart in favor of the mind when discussing worldview. But James K. A. Smith has helped to keep a person's desires central in our understanding of worldview. According to Smith (2009), we are first and foremost *desiring* beings, as opposed to *thinking* beings. I don't want to split hairs here between these two ideas. It is enough to say that we must keep a person's desires and inclinations at the forefront when we're working to nurture his or her worldview.

2. "Can Be Expressed as a Story or in a Set of Presuppositions Which We Hold about the Basic Constitution of Reality"

While a worldview begins with a bending of the heart toward some ultimate reality, it also will include an overarching narrative which sets the context for one's life and one's perspective of reality (Naugle, 2002). Sire (2015) calls these narratives "orienting patterns," which may be more or less cohesive and logical. As we mentioned in chapter 1, the orienting pattern for a biblical worldview is *Creation, Fall, Redemption, Restoration* (or *ought, is, can, will*). Also, a worldview will include a set of truth claims or a body of knowledge that claims to accurately represent the way things really are (Moreland, 2007).[6]

Don't be fooled by the word *set* in the previous sentence. I know that calling a person's deeply held assumptions (truth claims) about reality a set can lead one to believe it's an organized, logical system of thought. A set, however, can also be a random assemblage of items, like a wrench, a rusty key, and a bottle of nail polish in a kitchen junk drawer. It's a set in the sense that the stuff is all grouped in the same place. But it doesn't mean they go together logically. Sadly, I find that, for many Christians, the set of ideas that make up the cognitive dimension of their worldview resembles a junk drawer more than a well-organized silverware drawer, with every piece neatly laid out in appropriate places.

When discussing worldview, the facet we often think of first is a person's story of the world, or the presuppositions that a person holds to be true. Presuppositions or truth claims are relatively easy to identify and evaluate. As a result, we can be tempted to stop at them when examining a worldview. But when we do so, ignoring desire and behavior as components of a person's worldview, we only grasp one facet of worldview, and we neglect the whole story.

This shortfall is most evident in worldview assessments or survey instruments. Since it's hard to adequately assess a person's actual desires or behaviors through questions and answers on a test, most surveys measure one's agreement or disagreement with a set of truth claims in order to classify or label the person's worldview. This is helpful to ascertain a person's worldview and is a great prompt for people who take such surveys to begin thinking intentionally and methodically about their own worldview. But it reflects only one of the three dimensions. Results from such surveys should be treated as just one part of a bigger picture.

It's actually quite difficult to definitively classify someone's worldview. One time when I was discussing my research in worldview development with Dr. David Naugle from Dallas Baptist University, he lamented that probably the only way to really know a person's worldview would be to invite that person to live with you for a significant chunk of time. While that's certainly not practical in most cases, I agree with Dr. Naugle. But don't worry, I'm not going to suggest that your tenth grade Western Civ class move in with you. (However, as I said earlier, I will suggest that you should look at your class periods less as forty or fifty minutes in which to transfer and assess class content and more as precious time you get to live with your students. More on that later.)

3. "And That Provides the Foundation on Which We Live and Move and Have Our Being"

While the first two dimensions of a person's worldview are hard to see, the third is where everything is laid bare—in a person's actions. My worldview is most accurately displayed in my behaviors, which includes what I say and what I do. As James Sire says (2015, p. 153), "our worldview is not precisely what we state it to be. It is what is actualized in our behavior." The alignment of our behavior with our heart's desires and our cognitively held beliefs is a significant aspect of a maturing worldview.

> A person's behavior would never be a surprise to us if we truly knew their heart.

Dallas Willard asserts that a person's behavior would never be a surprise to us if we truly knew their heart (2002). Willard's view, rooted in biblical truth claims as articulated by Christ in Matthew 5:18, is that a person's behavioral habits flow naturally out of the heart. That is, behavior (in this case, a person's speech) is a reflection of what is going on in the heart.

Ideally, one's heart is well cultivated with good and virtuous desires that properly fuel an accurate understanding of the world and result in good and virtuous behaviors. More often, unfortunately, our behaviors evidence a disordered heart (or a heart oriented around one or more inferior visions of the good life) and inaccurate conceptions of reality.

WORLDVIEWS IN ACTION

To illustrate each of these dimensions and how they interact, consider how they could be lived out in the life of someone who subscribes to secularism, one of the chief worldviews that vies for our students' loyalty. As I discussed earlier, secularism drives the public education system. Remember, secularism views the world through the filter of atheism. There is no supernatural God of any kind, the physical cosmos is all that has ever existed, and everything that is has sprung up from purely physical, unguided processes. Secularism also views all religious experience as a private matter.

Let's assume that a specific secularist has a heart orientation toward success, the concept or ideal around which she orders her life. With success as the central, organizing desire of life, she will likely interpret all her experiences, and often the experiences of others, through a success-saturated story. The story of the world she "reads" will revolve around wealth: how people have gotten, lost, used, or otherwise interacted with money. It's as if she will have money-colored decoder glasses on, where everything she looks at will have the tint of wealth.

She will also believe a whole series of truth claims that energize and reinforce her desire for success. For example, she may hold the following to be true:

- Success is measured in terms of my financial wealth and its many benefits to me. Therefore, the more money and things I possess, the more successful I am.
- People who are not successful (by my measure) are of less value than those who are successful.
- It's okay for me to bend rules in order to achieve success.

- If someone else bends the rules in a way that negatively impacts my chances at success, it's not okay.
- Sometimes I need to sacrifice lesser ideals for the sake of my success.

With these ideas feeding her core desire for success, it is likely she will make choices about what to say and do that give (in her estimation) the best chances of attaining success. She may or may not be aware that she orders her behaviors in that way.

Generally, individuals and societies are not aware that they (1) are ordering their behaviors in certain ways, (2) have potentially contradictory and untrue ideas to which they subscribe, and (3) are pursuing their vision of the good life. It's as if they are simply anchored to and animated by an unexamined, unseen foundation and wellspring of life (think of Kant's super-sensible substrate).

> A person's worldview is the lens through which he or she interacts with the world. It includes core desires, underlying assumptions about what is true, and behavioral patterns that reflect desires and assumptions.

Of course, in the short space of this chapter, we can't delve into how her unique personality or life situation would impact her behaviors or craft a perfectly accurate description of how she would act in each and every circumstance. But we can agree she would make bigger-picture and everyday decisions that will bring her closer to her ultimate aim of being wealthy. She'll choose a college she believes will give her the best chances of landing a well-paying job after she graduates. She'll determine which job offer to take, based primarily on salary considerations. She'll befriend people at work who are most likely (in her estimation) to be in a position to help her move ahead. Her behaviors will reflect decisions she believes will move her along the continuum toward the kind of wealth she aspires to. This can even be in the small day-to-day decisions about how to treat others, what sort of attitude she'll have in relation to others' success or failure, and what kind of media she will consume—all of which are *behaviors*.

As this brief look into a secularist's life demonstrates, a person's worldview is the lens through which he or she interacts with the world. It includes core desires, underlying assumptions about what is true, and behavioral patterns that reflect desires and assumptions. As Kant taught, our worldview is often unseen or unnoticed. But it is the anchoring substance of our life and feeds every facet of who we are and what we do.

We've looked briefly at how a secularist's worldview animates and guides their life. But what about a person with a biblical worldview? In the next chapter, we'll examine this critical question.

CHAPTER 4

THE CENTER
POINT

When referring to a biblical worldview, we mean an organized framework of desires, assumptions, and habits that are submitted to Christ. The core desire that would motivate a person with a biblical worldview is a commitment to "seek first the kingdom [or rulership] of God" (Matthew 6:33). The central truth claims in a biblical worldview are (1) that God exists and (2) that God is who he has revealed himself to be in creation, the Bible, and the person of Jesus Christ (Phillips et al., 2008). A biblical worldview offers a unifying, ultimate desire. An expansive and complete set of biblical truth claims gives meaning and purpose to the full range of human experience, all of which leads to a consistent way of living, moving, and being.

THE LENS THROUGH WHICH WE SEE ALL ELSE

C. S. Lewis offered a helpful analogy for a biblical worldview when he said, "I believe in Christianity as I believe that the sun has risen: not only because I see it, but because by it I see everything else" (Martindale and Root, 1990, 99). Looking at all of creation and human history through the lens of a biblical worldview is like looking around on a sunny day; everything is illuminated and seen for what it truly is. This illuminating, immersive character of a biblical worldview is supported by Scriptures that affirm Christ as the source of all wisdom and knowledge and Christ himself as Truth.

> Looking at all of creation and human history through the lens of a biblical worldview is like looking around on a sunny day; everything is illuminated and seen for what it truly is.

When considered as a whole, a biblical worldview can be organized according to the narrative we briefly examined in chapter 1: *Creation, Fall, Redemption,* and *Restoration.* The central ideas behind this big-picture story are that God has a purpose for his creation, and that all things are moving along in the direction of his ultimate end. According to Colossians 1:20, God is reconciling to himself all things through the redemptive work of Christ. This is God's idea of "the good life." For the Christian, all our individual and broader human experiences are tied to this four-part story. An easier way to remember the parts of this story is to use the four smaller words we mentioned that represent the substance of each of the big words: *ought, is, can,* and *will.*

1. Creation/Ought

Creation represents the way things *ought* to be. Prior to Adam and Eve's sin, they lived in perfect fellowship with God, creation, and each other. This was how God designed humans to live. Had it not been for their fateful choice to go outside God's gracious provision of all things for them, they would still be living as truly *great* grandparents of a perfect and full world.

In their prefall state, Adam and Eve were given their assignment from God. They were to multiply, fill the earth, and subdue it. In essence, they were to be rulers in God's stead, regents over all creation. Many have called this assignment the creation mandate. It includes wrestling all of raw creation into a state of submission for good and godly purposes. Humans were designed to be God's vice-regents on earth. The work of stewarding creation was sweet before the fall and was an expression of intimate partnership with God as the owner of creation. This is the way things *ought* to be.

2. Fall/Is

But alas, the multidimensional, perfect communion enjoyed in the garden of Eden did not last. It was jarringly disrupted by Adam and Eve's assertion of self-rule against submission to God—what we have come to know as the fall of man. Before the fall, they desired God's rule. In the fall, they asserted their own rule, which was a voluntary assent to slavery under the rule of Satan. As a result of our first human parents' choice, the entire fabric of creation was altered in ways that continue to degrade. Adam and Eve were living in an environment ideally suited to human flourishing (immersed in a God-shaped worldview). Their sin ripped a gaping hole in the good boundary around that ideal environment, and a crushing and foul tsunami invaded every corner of their reality. From that time on, all their children (including us) would live and breathe in that new environment, ruthlessly invaded by death and sin. While God remained active in his creation, humans were profoundly separated from the quality of communion experienced in Eden (fueled by pure desire for God and his rulership). They would ultimately die apart from that communion.

The fall polluted every aspect of God's good creation, from man's ability to reason to his ability to live a full life in fellowship with God. While many things are still beautiful and still reflect the attributes of God (Romans 1), everything is marred by the impact of sin and separation from God. This is the *is* we currently experience. And all of us intuit that something is not right with the way life is, whether our worldview is secularism, postmodernism, new spirituality, Marxism, Islam, or Christianity (the six major competing worldviews of our day). Wolves eat lambs. Children die of incurable diseases. Hurricanes and earthquakes wipe out entire population centers. Families are torn apart by selfish choices. Churches and schools are targets of hateful individuals, hell-bent on destruction. No one who holds to any of these worldviews would suggest that these tragedies show that things are moving in the right direction. To the contrary, all of these are evidence of the pervasive and devastating effects of the new environment we live in. This is our *is*.

3. Redemption/Can

But hope is not lost, though, as John Milton famously said, *paradise* is. Even so, God has provided in Christ a way for his gracious rule to be reintroduced to a fallen and desperate humanity. Things *can* be different, and this is the defining centerpiece of the biblical worldview in terms of how it can impact the way things are. We are not permanent victims of creation gone awry. In the death and resurrection of Christ, he defied and conquered the ultimate elements of the postfall environment—sin and its companion, death. Because of Christ, all things *can* be made new and restored to the way they *ought* to be. As Albert Wolters says, "What was formed in creation has been historically deformed by sin and must be reformed in Christ" (Wolters, 1985, p. 76).

> The most glorious impact of Christ's redemptive work is that mankind can be restored to right relationship with God, the power that can flow into every other relationship and endeavor.

The most glorious impact of Christ's redemptive work is that mankind can be restored to right relationship with God, the power that can flow into every other relationship and endeavor. The sin- and self-saturated environment in which we live and move and have our being can be robbed of its deepest impact. And humans can experience a renewed and Eden-like relationship with God.

4. Restoration/Will

We have hope in our current state that things *can* be different. But a natural question that follows this truth claim is *will* they be different? Just because something *can* happen doesn't mean it *will*. A biblical worldview doesn't merely provide meaning and purpose for people who live in the distorted version of creation in which we live. It also provides a unique vision for a fundamental and comprehensive restoration of humanity and all other things to their prefall *ought*. Through the promise of a new creation, all things are fully restored to Christ. This means there is a day coming when the sin- and death-marred environment in which we live will be discarded in favor of a completely renewed creation—not unlike the experience of a caterpillar transforming into a completely new creature.

So how does all this find expression in the life of someone who has a biblical worldview? Just like our secularist friend, a person with a biblical worldview will live consistently with a unifying set of desires, truth claims, and behavioral patterns. In this case, however, the super-sensible substrate that anchors and nourishes life is one that conforms to the bedrock of Scripture. Since this book focuses on Christian education, let's look at how a biblical worldview will be expressed in the life of a Christian teacher.

TEACHING FROM A BIBLICAL WORLDVIEW

As we've already seen, heart orientation is the starting place for a worldview. A worldview anchored and nourished by Scripture will be first and foremost concerned with what God desires for his people. In Matthew 6:33, Jesus cut through all the competing desires that we can have. Our core heart orientation should be the kingdom of God. Having this as a chief desire cancels out any lesser desire that takes first place.

For a Christian teacher, to seek God's kingdom first means he will put God's agenda first in every interaction with students. It means he will approach every subject matter and every skill that needs to be taught from a kingdom-first perspective. If we return to our roots in Eden, we'll see that this means we serve as his stewards over creation, subduing, shaping, and using it in ways that demonstrate he is Lord of all things. We can take this thought too far in suggesting that we can achieve the fullness of his kingdom now through our own efforts. Even so, it is helpful for the Christian teacher to be consistently thinking, "How can I provide Eden-like experiences for my students?"

Of course, we are not fully free from the impact of the curse. According to the biblical narrative we examined earlier, we won't be free until the final restoration of all things. But that doesn't mean we can't purposefully shape our students' environment to have many elements of the *ought* of Eden. Teachers with a biblical worldview will strive to do that, relying on the empowerment of Christ's Holy Spirit, who lives in them. He can animate even the most mundane aspects of teaching and learning. This is how a properly oriented core desire for God's rulership forms the foundation for the Christian teacher's worldview. Such a teacher will make all decisions about what to do in the classroom and about how to interact with students from this starting point.

I often find that teachers in Christian schools have veered off course at this starting point. This is especially true when a teacher has what Francis Schaeffer (1981) calls a "two-story" view of reality, which is often picked up more by default than design. This is how many individuals in our culture—and unfortunately in our secular, teacher-training institutions—view reality.

To illustrate the negative impact of this sacred/secular divide, Schaeffer often referenced a two-story house. Many in today's society believe that a person's values and beliefs reside in the upper story, while facts and hard science dwell in the lower story. It's fine to have values and beliefs that are consistent with Scripture—just keep them neatly tucked away in the upper story like nostalgic heirlooms in the attic. They certainly can't have meaningful bearing on the lower story where we have to get serious about life and preparing our students for the real world.

I've worked with some delightful and skilled teachers who love Christ and his Word. But they somehow separate that love from the work they do as teachers. It's not that they're actively working against bringing a "seek first his kingdom" orientation to their teaching. It's just that they see that as separate, a Sunday or personal discipleship thing, as opposed to an everyday school thing.

Most teachers in Christian schools have not spent a single day as a student in an educational environment that seeks to keep God's kingdom first. To the contrary, at best, they've been trained in institutions that take a two-story view of reality. In such an institution, aspiring teachers will learn that their personal spiritual values are fine as long as they are kept private, because they have no appropriate place in science, math, or language arts. Or at worst, they're trained in a militant, anti-kingdom posture. They'll be told that it is the height of folly to orient one's life around a transcendent God, which borders on educational malpractice.

As Francis Schaeffer said, "It is very difficult to live … as a college or university student for four years or longer and not become infiltrated by the surrounding worldview" (Schaeffer, 1984, p. 120). This secular indoctrination takes some time and effort to detox out of a teacher's system. Unfortunately, this is the way most teachers are trained in the US, and sadly, this is also true for Christian institutions. There are only a few Christian colleges that have any sort of program emphasis on teaching in Christian schools (Stoner, 2012). This means that virtually none of us have been intentionally prepared for providing our students with an experience of immersion in a biblical worldview.

A teacher with a biblical worldview will live and teach from the center point of desiring God's kingdom first. But that's only the starting place. Students

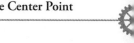

need to have not only their desires shaped but their thoughts as well. Thankfully, Scripture informs us of this facet of a teacher's work too.

SHAPING THOUGHTS

Perhaps the most iconic biblical reference to the concept of shaping thoughts is found in 2 Corinthians 10:5. Paul describes a deeply spiritual process that occurs in the domain of cognition. Cognition, or thinking, occurs in the mind. To think is to hold a given idea (or series of ideas) in the mind. To consider, use, or evaluate them is the process of deciding whether to hold them as true. Paul talks about this process in terms that specifically relate to God's kingdom. He says every thought must be taken captive to Christ. Every idea, whether about arithmetic, genetics, or music theory, should be examined to determine if it is submitted to Christ. Concepts that are consistent with Christ's view of reality can stay. The ones that aren't should be banished from active influence on the mind because they are unfit representations of the way things actually are. Thoughts that can stay as a result of being found to be true are the ones Christian teachers will gladly introduce to their students. Ones that can't stay because they aren't true should be classified as such and discarded as unreliable building blocks for a student's growing worldview. Christian teachers won't shy away from developmentally appropriate exposure to false ideas. But they'll be careful to guide students to think correctly about those ideas.

This way of looking at the Christian teacher's approach to engaging content moves a teacher past being a dispenser of information to becoming a guide in discernment. And this begins with even the youngest learners. For example, take an important core thought that is part of a Christian worldview and that is highly relevant in today's culture. Abortion is morally wrong because it ends an innocent human life. How might a Christian preschool teacher deliver this content to a four-year-old?

That's perhaps an unfair question, because everyone knows you wouldn't do a lesson on abortion with a group of four-year-olds. However, Christian teachers who understand the Lord is using them to shape the desires, thoughts, and actions of students in developmentally appropriate ways will not settle for merely discussing shapes, colors, and letters. They will also create opportunities to lay foundation stones in students' minds that will one day be combined with more complex thoughts. Doing that will enable them to arrive at a mature understanding of God's perspective on abortion. Teachers do this in subtle but important ways.

A common occurrence in the preschool classroom is the celebration of a new sibling. Teachers with a biblical worldview will intentionally add specific truths to the celebration:

- "Isn't it amazing how God is creating a sister or brother for Susan?"
- "Did you know that the Bible tells us that all babies are a gift from God?"
- "Let's pray for Susan's mommy today. Right now, God is at work creating a new little brother or sister in her tummy!"

As this simple example demonstrates, you can be intentional about introducing and expanding concepts and ideas that are true to your students, no matter the grade level. Obviously, if you're teaching twelfth graders, the discussion about abortion can and should require much more robust thinking and processing.

What we're discussing here applies to more than just the hot-button moral issues of our day. Here's where we really get into the difference a biblical worldview makes in the practice of a Christian teacher. God's view on abortion is fairly easy to discern. But what does he think about physics or chemistry or Latin, and what thoughts in these subject areas need to be submitted to Christ?

INTERACTING WITH TRUTH CLAIMS

Remember, anything that is true (an accurate representation of the way things actually are) can stay. Claims or statements that aren't true can't. So one way of looking at teaching from a Christian worldview could be seen as guiding students to examine, understand, and use what is true. This broad description of teaching takes our focus off delivering content and moves our attention to the bigger purpose of effectively interacting with truth claims. We help our students know and faithfully use what is true in service of a consuming desire to seek first his kingdom.

In this way of thinking, we get away from the lowest level of biblical integration. Dr. Bryan Smith (2019), of Bob Jones University Press, has described various levels of biblical integration: *relegation, referencing, responding,* and *rebuilding.* While we are discussing immersion as opposed to integration, Smith's work is still helpful in keeping us from the lowest levels of integration.

In the lowest level, truth claims from Scripture are *relegated* to prayer time, devotions, chapel, Bible class, and such. *Referencing* is turning to Scripture for illustrations and examples in class. For instance, in a discussion of the properties and usage of wool, the teacher points to Gideon's fleece or the fact that Christ is our Good

Shepherd. (And, yes, these uses of Scripture have a way of feeling contrived and too much like two-story thinking.)

Responding is the use of Scripture as the key criteria in evaluating truths and using those truths in positive ways, such as writing letters to the local government to address a problem in the community. Dr. Smith's final level is *rebuilding*, which refers to the grand project of redeeming every topic in every academic subject area to rebuild understanding in these areas from a distinctly biblical perspective. Christian teachers whose primary desire is the kingdom of God will see their role as moving students along this continuum to the point where every subject area has been brought into submission to Christ.

Teachers with a biblical worldview will not be satisfied, though, with merely a biblically faithful approach to content. They will also have a consuming conviction that "faith without works is dead." While this may seem obvious, desiring the kingdom and thinking thoughts that are aligned with the kingdom without practical fruit is, well, fruitless. The shaping of desire and thought must have application to one's behavior. And by this, I don't just mean a legalistic set of moral dictates, though certainly a student's (and a teacher's) moral behavior should be guided by Scripture. I'm talking about seeing our individual story as a part of the overarching narrative I described earlier. Each human being can be equipped to engage in restoring all things. I like to call this worldview-aligned behavior *applied* biblical worldview. I'll offer four helpful questions that can lead us and our students to active engagement in restoring all things—the real-world fruit of a biblical worldview.

> Each human being can be equipped to engage in restoring all things.

FOUR QUESTIONS FROM AN APPLIED BIBLICAL WORLDVIEW

In their book, *Restoring All Things*, John Stonestreet and Warren Smith (2015) document dozens of stories about people, local institutions, and ministries actively working to restore some small slice of reality to the way things ought to be. From Christian crisis pregnancy centers encouraging young moms to carry their babies to term and helping them to raise those babies well, to innovative Christian-owned businesses delivering excellent products and services to the glory of God, everyday people are changing the world through living out the implications of a biblical worldview in their own little (or big) sphere of influence.

To introduce the stories they tell, Smith and Stonestreet suggest an organizing framework within which those small-scale and small-town heroes are operating—a series of four questions. Since I love alliteration, I've adapted each of their questions to include a key *C* word and hopefully make them easier to recall in the process.

1. What Is Good in our Culture That We Can *Cultivate?*

The first question is, "What is good in our culture that we can *cultivate?*" According to our earlier discussion about the state of creation after the fall of man, things have gotten really bad—but not *totally* bad. In fact, there's still quite a bit of good in the culture and in nature that can be cultivated. Outside of agriculture, the word *cultivate* generally means to improve, refine, or develop, such as in cultivating a taste for classical music or cultivating one's mind through rigorous study. (Right now, for instance, you are cultivating the ability to immerse your students in a biblical worldview!)

Looking at the culture around us, there's plenty that's good. Music, art, buildings, sports—the list of things and activities that are good could go on endlessly. Assessing whether or not things are good hearkens back to God's original assessment of his wonderful creation—that it was "good." Indeed there's much good in what God and humans—the crown of his creation—have created. And all that is good can still be made better or cultivated. Musicians can always improve. Soccer players can get better. Businesses can be run more efficiently and with more human compassion. Buildings can be more beautiful. And teenage boys' bedrooms can be tidier. All this relates to this first question of how we as Christians can cultivate what's already here to make it better.

2. What Is Missing in Our Culture That We Can *Create*?

The second question is, "What is missing in our culture that we can *create*?" I suppose the word *create* here is a bit dramatic, but I like it because it connects us deeply to God's creative work. Sure, we can creatively *contribute* things that are missing (as Smith and Stonestreet phrase their question), but there's something deeply meaningful to me in the word *create*.

Maybe I also like the word *create* because I'm a carpenter. I grew up working summers and school vacations with my dad. For several years as a young adult, I was a carpenter in my father's construction business. I guess you could say carpentry was my destiny. When most kids were playing video games, as a teenager I was out swinging a hammer and cutting two-by-fours. I couldn't help but become a carpenter, I suppose. I truly love building, whether it's a complete house or a new dining room table. To me, there's just about nothing better than driving up to a construction site to find piles of wood waiting for me to create something of worth, usefulness, and beauty.

This is the creative spirit we all share and which we as Christians should be living out every day. It may be creating a piece of furniture, blazing a new frontier in an area of knowledge, generating a solution to a thorny problem, or creating warmth or acceptance in our relational environments. An applied biblical worldview means we consistently look for things we can create.

> An applied biblical worldview means we consistently look for things we can create.

3. What Is Broken That We Can *Cure*?

Question number three is, "What is broken that we can *cure*?" If the first two questions seem a bit optimistic, this one brings us back to the reality of the *is* in which we currently live. While spiritual redemption through Christ is available to humans, there is also an awful lot in our culture and our world that is, well, awful. I'm not yet talking about what's truly evil; we'll get to that in our next framing question. When God looks at contemporary culture, he says about many things, "It is *not* good." And so should we. But more than just making a statement about the terrible way things are, we are to do something about those things.

When we think about all the things that are not good in our culture, it's common to begin with the biggies. Broken political systems. Broken societal morals. Broken financial markets. But let's begin with the simple things that aren't good. We don't need to walk far in the halls of even the best Christian schools to find things that are not good. A student who feels alone. A door that doesn't close right or a gash in a wall. An upperclassman with anxiety about college decisions. From personal brokenness to brokenness in the physical building, there's plenty to be cured right in our own schools. Students can be challenged and expected to be a part of the cures that are needed.

Thinking ahead to what our students will do in the future, entire vocations are based upon this idea of curing what is not good. While the medical field may be an obvious venue in which to practice curing, many professions line up with this concept. Consultants help cure sick organizations or projects. Asphalt layers cure bad roads. Appliance repairmen cure sick dishwashers.

I hope you picked up my philosophy of good and not good. I'm not merely thinking in terms of what is or is not *morally* good. I just haven't mentioned many of those examples, because I believe that we Christians can limit our curing activities too easily. Certainly, I believe things which are morally bad need curing, such as abortion, the sex trade, drug abuse, and the like. We'll get to those kinds of issues in the next framing question. However, I see an applied biblical worldview as extending to *all* of God's creation and to every facet that is not the way it ought to be. You may feel like I'm really pushing this concept. But think about how having this perspective could invigorate so much of what we routinely do—things we often dread.

Not long after buying her first car, my daughter discovered that it needed new struts. No, I was not happy at first. But with an applied biblical worldview, the situation takes on a whole new ethos. Instead of dreading the repair I needed to make, I could think in terms of curing what's not good with Hannah's car. I got to take something that was broken (not good) and make it good and restore it to proper function. Not only that, I got to do it with my son, who I'm training to be self-sufficient when it comes to car repairs. Really, *this isn't just spin*. Approaching our day-to-day opportunities to make not-good things good helps to immerse all of life in God's way of looking at reality. How can you extend this idea into your work as a teacher?

4. What Is Evil in Our Culture That We Can *Curb*?

Our final question gets at what's ultimately wrong with creation: "What is evil in our culture that we can *curb*?" This one brings us to the front lines of the cosmic battle between God's good plan for humanity and Satan's age-old rebellion against the rulership of God. To curb means to restrain or put a check on something. Just a quick look at the culture around us provides ample examples of the rampant evil that's been wreaking havoc throughout creation since the fall. Things aren't just broken; they're fundamentally skewed away from God. And we can play a role in holding back the seemingly relentless tide of evil.

An applied biblical worldview leads us to not merely lament the evil machinations of mankind, but to actually work to curb them.

> Things aren't just broken; they're fundamentally skewed away from God. And we can play a role in holding back the seemingly relentless tide of evil.

But you may ask, "How can students in my Christian school take on evil?" Sure, it can be overwhelming to think about *all* the evil in the world, but that's not where we need to start. What about the evil in our school? Think about it: if you accept the biblical concept that mankind is in rebellion to God's good rulership, that includes the representatives of mankind that sit in your classrooms and walk your hallways. I'm certainly not suggesting that all your students do evil things all the time. But whenever a student is marginalized by the more popular students or a student cheats on an assignment, evil is at work in your school.

My personal experience is that this is one of the big challenges our Christian students face. They have a hard time taking on this kind of local evil. A student may be incensed at the reality of abortion, but not say anything when a peer obviously copies an answer from a friend or tries alcohol on the senior trip. Not long ago, we had an issue in our school where several students participated in an evil activity together. We talked with students who were at the event and had firsthand knowledge of what happened. I was disheartened by the lack of boldness of our students to actively curb or restrain the evil they knew was going on.

My suggestion here is to constantly cast the vision for curbing evil among our students. This applies both in the biggies that prominently plague our culture and in the smaller-scale evil that manifests in the everyday interactions among our students. A student who lovingly confronts a friend with a habit of using profanity and the one who participates in the annual March for Life are both working to curb evil.

Focusing on these four questions in our interactions with students helps keep a biblical worldview from being ineffective and from devolving into being merely a set of truth propositions we say we believe.

Now that we've explored how to define a worldview, the three dimensions of a worldview, the general shape of a biblical worldview, and the nature of an applied biblical worldview, several major questions remain. The first of these is how does a biblical worldview take shape in a person? Our next chapter will explore this by looking at some exciting current research in the field of biblical worldview development.

CHAPTER 5

HOW A BIBLICAL
WORLDVIEW
TAKES SHAPE

The gathering storm in Middle-earth is ominous. Leaders from that mythical realm assemble in Rivendell to discuss their options. In the course of their deliberations, Frodo places the One Ring on a stand in the center of the gathering. It becomes clear someone will need to make the trek into Mordor to destroy this emblem of hideous power. In a memorable statement of truth laced with desperation, Boromir of Gondor interjects, "One does not simply walk into Mordor."

This classic scene in *The Fellowship of the Ring* prompted countless memes based on Boromir's words. "One does not simply …" sets up countless statements of the unstated obvious.

The way Christian schools approach the idea of biblical world-view could lead one to think that by just adding a few

ingredients—poof—"one simply walks into a biblical worldview." But it's not that simple, especially if a biblical worldview is much more than just being able to repeat a set of truth propositions consistent with Scripture. As we discussed earlier, this is only one part of a biblical worldview.

Several years ago, I set out to discover how to develop Sire's three-dimensional biblical worldview (heart orientation, truth propositions, behavioral alignment). First I scoured resources in print and on the internet to see if there was a model for biblical worldview development already available. While many authors hinted at how a worldview develops, I could find no one who had devised an overall developmental model for how that happens. It just wasn't there.

In the course of my doctoral work, I decided to do the research myself. To make it doable, I started with what many people believe is a critical stage in human development—the emerging adult years. I think it's easy to see how important the years between eighteen and twenty-three are when considering worldview development. Numerous national ministries support emerging adults as they develop their worldview. The span between the ages of eighteen and twenty-three is the hinge upon which a person's entire life turns. With so many young adults walking away from biblical faith once they leave home, the stakes for discerning what's going on during this life stage are hugely important. If we could understand the processes emerging adults experienced as they developed their worldview, we could better prepare younger teens and children for that same journey.

I spent hundreds of hours talking with a group of amazing Christian young adults about their experiences. Then, thinking deeply about what I learned from them, I created a pictorial representation of how a biblical worldview develops during the early emerging adult years. You'll notice that I didn't create a timeline. That just didn't seem to capture the holistic process I was investigating. Gears seemed to be more appropriate.

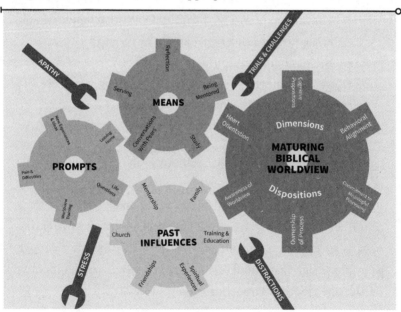

Biblical worldview development in the emerging adult years is not linear or step by step. It is a complex interplay of experiences and the means by which emerging adults process those experiences, all tempered and impacted by their past. To develop my ideas, I worked with some of the most promising emerging adults. They were the kind of individuals all our schools want to produce. What I found was not surprising. But it was profound and suggested many areas in which Christian schools—and Christian schoolteachers—can improve.

INFLUENCES FROM THE PAST

Emerging adults with a strong biblical worldview don't just show up after high school with a blank worldview slate. Their worldview has been impacted by their childhood and teen experiences and particularly positive shaping influences:

- growing up in strong, evangelical Christian families
- being involved in a local church
- having significant spiritual experiences
- participating in biblical worldview training
- enjoying positive Christian friendships
- being mentored by Christian adults

Most of these factors that can positively shape our students are out of our control. However, even without those factors, we can influence our students toward them. Additionally, some of these factors are directly in our control, and we'll discuss these later. For now, as we explore how a biblical worldview develops, it is enough to acknowledge that childhood and teen experiences significantly impact one's journey through emerging adulthood.

NEW EXPERIENCES/PROMPTS

Emerging adulthood is filled with opportunities to see new things and be confronted with decisions for which the individual is now fully responsible, the stuff of "adulting." For those who worked with me in my research, these new experiences became important prompts for growth. These prompts included

- leaving home,
- encountering new ideas,
- engaging in worldview training,
- facing pain or difficulties, and
- considering big questions about life.

But just experiencing new things does not make a person grow. Growth in a biblical worldview depends on whether a person processes (reflects on, considers, evaluates) those new experiences. Remember the famous maxim attributed to Socrates? "The unexamined life is not worth living." This is particularly relevant for emerging adults who are intent upon developing a biblical worldview. They cannot simply drift from new experience to new experience and expect to develop a biblical worldview. They must intentionally process their experiences.

Processing is an umbrella term for the ways in which a person mulls over, considers, and attaches meaning to experiences, which is largely what worldview development is all about. As I'll unpack more later in this chapter, biblical worldview development is an intentional process. It doesn't just happen by osmosis, though much of the foundational desires, thoughts, and actions can be "caught." Emerging adults with a solid biblical worldview mull over what they experience. Then they make well-considered decisions about what those experiences mean and how they should respond to them, both immediately and with new or enhanced habits.

One example of how this plays out comes from my friend Phil (not his real name), a pastoral studies major. Between his junior and senior years of college, he interned in an area where he'd never been before. He was exposed to the new dynamics of living and working with people he didn't know. One of the elements of the church culture in that area was the easy acceptance of alcohol. He was from a denomination that had a strong stance against any alcohol consumption. Phil was shocked when the church leadership team went out for beers after a meeting.

Phil was unsettled in his heart and mind and was in a bit of a tailspin. However, instead of just having a to-each-his-own attitude, he engaged the issue with study, prayer, deep consideration, and conversations with friends and mentors. There was certainly a disorienting gap between his initial experience and the day when things settled for him. But looking back, he classifies this as an opportunity to deepen his own roots and to understand why he held the personal standards he held. He clearly sees his struggle and the resulting engagement of the alcohol issue as a key formative season in his worldview. This not only helped him settle the alcohol question, but also gave him real-world experience in processing through a disorienting new experience.

> At every level, we can help our students learn to process experiences in ways that will prepare them for the critical years of biblical worldview development. It starts with creating opportunities for our students to experience new things.

I hope you're beginning to see ways to craft processing experiences for your students. Processing is absolutely key to intentional worldview development. At every level, we can help our students learn to process experiences in ways that will prepare them for the critical years of biblical worldview development. It starts with creating opportunities for our students to experience new things. Then we can support them in age-appropriate ways to think through, reflect, and mull over their experience. Then they will arrive at conclusions about what those experiences mean and about how those conclusions should impact what they desire, think, and do.

PROCESSING EXPERIENCES

The emerging adults who worked with me in my research were not a group of friends who could compare notes prior to our conversations. However, they consistently pointed to several common ways of processing their life experiences:

- conversations with peers
- reflection
- study
- being mentored
- serving others

Reflect for a few minutes on how you might immerse your students in an opportunity-rich learning environment to process new experiences. Identify the processing you already require of your students. Then attach greater meaning and motivation to that processing. For instance, most English teachers already require some kind of regular journal writing. Consider how you may harness what you're already doing to give your students practice in the worldview development processing they'll rely upon throughout their lifetime.

By far, the most common means of processing experiences for my friends was talking with peers. Time after time, they said that when they hit unfamiliar territory in life, their method for making sense of it all was to talk with friends. Today's emerging adults long for real friendships—relational contexts in which they can talk about what's happening in life and explore ideas and feelings out loud.

Beyond peer discussions, though, they also spent time studying, often by searching out information from the internet and books. While most emerging adults I've talked to (even beyond my research project) still prefer actual books over e-books for in-depth reading, the internet is their go-to method for first-level information and input when they are faced with a conundrum.

Some people talk about the Gutenberg-to-Google' revolution as having already happened. But I wonder how many of our schools have taken seriously the need to help our students master the skill of finding reliable and useful information on the internet. My experience teaching undergraduate students suggests emerging adults are not very savvy when it comes to determining what's worthwhile and what's worthless in the wild and jumbled world of internet content.

The emerging adults in my project were also deeply reflective, meaning they spent time thinking about the things that troubled them or didn't make sense. These were not the kind of people who would just say, "Oh well . . . it is what it is." They wanted to know what *it* was and *why* it was what it was. They had a natural curiosity and were discontent with pat answers or shallow explanations.

Think carefully about that last statement. Maybe read it out loud a time or two, until the truth of it really strikes you. I hope our Christian schools are not brokering in pat answers and shallow explanations!

In the discussions with my young friends about how to understand new experiences, the concept of mentoring came up again, just as it had when we explored their childhood and teen influences. We often shortchange today's emerging adults, prejudging that they don't value the input of people who are older and wiser than they are. My research suggests this just isn't true. They actually crave mentors who can share their experiences with them. Just as importantly, they want their mentors to serve as wise sounding boards with whom they can talk about their own experiences.

Note, however, that mentoring is not exclusively about having all the right answers. Unfortunately, we often classify mentoring as a means to give younger people answers to all their questions. While there certainly will be opportunity to tell our students what they need to know, mentoring is a much more robust relationship that includes as much asking as it does telling. Dr. Jeff Myers (2010), in

> Effective mentoring involves asking great questions that prompt the other person to probe for the meaning in new experiences.

his book *Cultivate*, calls this facet of mentoring the "relational posture of coaching" (p. 76). Effective mentoring involves asking great questions that prompt the other person to probe for the meaning in new experiences. As team members in a Christian school, we can all be equipped with great question-asking skills. This applies to the headmaster who has quick hallway conversations with students, as well as the guidance counselor whose entire role revolves around preparing students to face new experiences in college and beyond.

Serving others also ranked high in the list of how emerging adults work through and understand the meaning of their experiences. Individuals involved in my research expressed that serving others through mentoring, coaching, and teaching teens and children was a key part of their own biblical worldview development. As the old adage goes, "You learn something best when you teach it to others." When an emerging adult is called upon to help someone younger process new information or experiences, the impact is not only felt in the younger one, but in the mentor as well.

DERAILERS

This biblical worldview development process is not without challenges. It's not a seamless flow from experience to processing and then on to new experiences. In truth, the whole process can be derailed by challenges that everyday life can toss into the works. Four primary derailers were identified by the emerging adults in my study:

- apathy
- stress
- distractions
- trials and pain

Not only did emerging adults have to be on guard against these potential obstacles, but they saw the profound impact of these on their peers—especially their peers who seemed to not have a well-developed biblical worldview.

Apathy is simply an "I don't care" or a "meh" attitude—kind of like a perpetual shrug of the shoulders. Stress is produced by the relentless demands that emerging adults face, from financial pressure and relational difficulties to academic deadlines. Distractions come in all kinds of forms, including social media, binge-watching shows, and other less-than-noble pursuits. Trials and pain can be just about anything that brings discomfort or legitimate suffering to life. Here's the bottom line on this: emerging adults who are purposefully developing their biblical worldview generally know how to manage derailers, and they actually do so. Individuals who aren't experiencing a thriving biblical worldview don't know how to manage them.

THREE DISPOSITIONS OF A MATURING BIBLICAL WORLDVIEW

We've discussed Sire's three dimensions—heart orientation, truth propositions, and behavioral alignment. Let's look now at the three dispositions. According to the Oxford English Dictionary, a disposition is a "natural tendency, a bend of the mind." An emerging adult (and by extension, anyone) with a maturing biblical worldview will demonstrate three important tendencies. They will be aware of their own worldview, be committed to meaningful processing, and take ownership of their own worldview development.

1. Awareness

Awareness means they know the contours of their own worldview. They know where it aligns with God's view of reality, how one should function within that reality, and where their own worldview still needs shaping.

Here's where I was really impacted by my findings. In my work with the exceptional emerging adults in my study, I found they were not convinced they actually had a fully developed biblical worldview. Instead, they acknowledged they had lots of growing to do. Rather than saying they had a *mature* biblical worldview, they classified themselves as having a *maturing* biblical worldview. It would seem then that an appropriate goal for this life stage is not a fully formed biblical worldview. Instead, it's dynamically growing and exhibits both Sire's three dimensions and the newly identified three dispositions of a biblical worldview.

2. Meaningful Processing

Meaningful processing refers to what we discussed earlier. Those with a maturing biblical worldview are not hapless victims of life. They are committed to consciously and actively processing their experiences.

3. Ownership

And finally, they don't hand the reins of their development over to others, as if it's someone else's job to make sure they grow. They willingly take responsibility for their own worldview development.

IMPLICATIONS FOR AN IMMERSIVE BIBLICAL WORLDVIEW EDUCATION

As I prodded earlier, I hope you're beginning to think about how this model for biblical worldview development should guide your teaching, whether you have a class full of fifteen preschoolers or whether you see eighty-five different high schoolers throughout the course of a day. In this section, we'll look at some implications of my research.

Part of providing an immersive worldview experience is understanding how a biblical worldview develops. We've only looked at one important life stage—emerging adulthood. But it is easy to work backward from this starting point to see how our work with younger students can be consistent with what we've learned.

1. Expected Student Outcomes

In a way, the emerging adults in my research group represent the ideals we in Christian schools look for in our graduates. They are consciously aware of their own worldview and they are actively working to develop it further. They had a strong foundation from their childhood and teenage years. And while they don't claim to have arrived, they truly are exemplary. Any Christian school would be proud to number them among their alumni. Elements of their profiles, as identified in my research, can serve as a set of ultimate student outcomes. Like any good educational initiative, we can work backward from our end goal to inform the kinds of learning spaces we will create for our students throughout their Christian school experience.

Let me list them for you here in one place, as if they were a formal set of expected student outcomes for a Christian school:

By the time our students graduate, they will

- be aware of their own worldview;
- be committed to actively processing new life experiences in meaningful ways;
- own the ongoing development of their worldview;
- identify the impact various childhood experiences have had on their worldview;
- have had multiple meaningful interactions with individuals who espouse various non-Christian worldviews;
- have had significant practice in processing new experiences through peer discussions, reflection, study, and prayer;
- have had at least one significant mentoring relationship with an individual who has a well-developed biblical worldview;
- have served in at least one teaching or mentoring context that provided the opportunity to serve individuals whose worldview is less developed;
- have participated in a minimum of one formal worldview course on the high school or college level;

- have learned effective strategies to manage stress, especially academic pressures, relationship challenges, and the expectations of others;
- have learned effective strategies to manage distractions, such as social media, entertainment, and so on;
- have embraced a biblical view of trials and difficulties;
- have demonstrated success in navigating trials and difficulties.

The good news is that this set of outcomes encompasses many concepts or experiences common to our Christian schools. You don't have to look far or long to find plenty of opportunities to help students manage stress or to prod them to face new experiences. A mind-set toward immersing your students in a biblical worldview will give new meaning and focus to even the most mundane (and sometimes the most frustrating) aspects of school. Remember, though, that biblical worldview development is a life-long process, and not something that happens in one year or in one class. Remember Boromir: One does not simply walk into a biblical worldview. Students' entire Christian school experience can and should be a series of experiences harnessed by all school personnel for worldview development.

2. Expected Teaching Obligations

Let's look at one simple example: teaching biblical financial management. In some Christian schools, this is an elective course or one unit in some broader course. However, many Christian schools don't require any course of this sort. How does this lack of training on biblical financial management impact students? Aside from the practical issue of setting them up for problems when they are responsible for managing their own finances, it's the secondary issue that concerns me—stress. We've all heard that money troubles contribute to all kinds of stress in life, from the slavery to debt to the conflict that money causes in many marriages. So it's logical to conclude that the stress of poor money management can be a major derailer when it comes to actively developing one's worldview. As one of my emerging adult friends said, "A lot of students just say, 'I don't know how to deal with all that's going on in life, so I don't even care about what I believe.'" What she is saying is that the stress of everyday living can easily crowd out a disciplined and focused effort to develop one's worldview.

This is a disturbing thought. While we're busy teaching classes on apologetics and comparative worldviews (which are both important), we may be ignoring something equally important. Our students are not likely to go on to develop a strong biblical worldview if their lives are absorbed with the corrosive effects of stress. I've known many *emerging* adults and in fact many *emerged* adults who lack the mental and spiritual reserves to devote any energy to proactive worldview development because their minds and hearts are consumed with overcoming financial straits.

Think about how to approach this issue from a worldview-development perspective. By teaching students how to manage money according to God's principles, you're doing so much more than equipping them with valuable life skills. You're actually helping to create a lifestyle friendly to developing a biblical worldview. You're investing in lives, which minimizes stress resulting from financial pressures. This thoroughly energizes me to focus attention on financial training for students of all ages, even well before they're ready for a semester-long class using Dave Ramsey's material.

> Everything we do can be harnessed in service of worldview development in our students and immerse them in a biblical worldview-rich environment.

This is just one example of how to think about the ultimate student outcomes I've suggested. We can work throughout a student's entire school experience to make meaningful deposits in their lives—deposits that can bear significant fruit throughout their lifetime of worldview development. Everything we do can be harnessed in service of worldview development in our students and immerse them in a biblical worldview-rich environment.

3. Team Development

I recommend having the entire school faculty and staff team study and understand each of these outcomes (and I mean the *entire* team—janitors, teacher aides, department chairpersons, coaches, *everyone*). Feel free to adapt and customize them in relation to your school's unique vision and mission. Next, encourage one another to do two specific things. First, all of us can leverage the power of everyday moments to contribute towards these ultimate outcomes. Second, we can intentionally plan learning spaces to be worldview-rich environments through *how we teach*. More on this in the second section of the book, which we'll get to soon. But first, we need a starting point that comes before your classroom—yourself.

CHAPTER 6

DEVELOPING YOUR OWN
WORLDVIEW

Bruce Lockerbie is a respected father in the Christian school movement. After a long and effective career as a teacher and coach at the famed Stony Brook School on Long Island (NY), he became a sought-after consultant. He has worked with hundreds of schools and thousands of Christian educators. Like the E. F. Hutton of the Christian school world, when Bruce Lockerbie talks, people listen.

I had the honor of living about ten miles from Lockerbie while I was head of a school on Long Island. We had many opportunities to talk over lunch or coffee. I learned much from his wisdom and wit. A pleasant gadfly (I think he'd be okay with that), Lockerbie is always prodding Christian educators to give our best efforts to cultivating in ourselves a biblical worldview. To Lockerbie, this is the nonnegotiable foundation for offering a truly Christian education.

In his book *A Christian Paideia: The Habitual Vision of Greatness*, Lockerbie says it this way: "We cannot overemphasize the importance of acquiring and representing a Christian worldview . . . For us as Christian educators, understanding the significance of a worldview is a matter of the greatest urgency and therefore ought to be the primary focus of our profession" (2005, p. 11). If you take what Lockerbie is saying seriously, you will devote your best efforts toward developing in yourself a biblical worldview, knowing that doing so is the key starting place for helping others do the same.

Back in chapter 1, I identified five key elements of a school that provides an immersive worldview experience for students. This chapter relates to element 1: *Teachers who are aware of and actively developing their worldview.* I'll be giving you practical, actionable advice on how you can further develop a biblical worldview.

AWARENESS OF THE THREE DIMENSIONS

It's important to remember that your worldview is more than what you know. It's also what you desire and how you act. All three of these dimensions work in concert with one another. So your efforts to develop this three-dimensional phenomenon need to honor each of these elements. You cannot focus all of your efforts on one dimension at the expense of the other two and expect to have a well-formed worldview.

> You cannot focus all of your efforts on one dimension at the expense of the other two and expect to have a well-formed worldview.

I've noticed that people tend to think first of the knowledge dimension when approaching the idea of developing their worldview. Often, they'll reach for a book or they'll find a conference without a plan for what they'll do with what they read or hear. They're looking for more information. This is important, but it's not the whole story. Unless it's paired with equal attention to cultivating their core desires and improving how they actually live, it leads to impoverished results. Even in writing this book, I risk encouraging you to just gain more knowledge about worldviews and worldview development. If you don't pair your learnings from what you read with efforts to shape your desires and your actions, we will have both failed.

With those warnings on record, let's begin to explore how to develop your own biblical worldview. Do you remember what we learned from how exemplary emerging adults develop their biblical worldview? Everything I'm suggesting related to practical application will be tied to the model of worldview development we've already discussed. This will keep our efforts anchored in how worldviews actually develop, as opposed to pursuing ideas that may or may not be grounded in reality.

FIVE PRINCIPLES FOR ACTIVE WORLDVIEW DEVELOPMENT

The primary engine for worldview development in exemplary emerging adults is a series of new experiences they faithfully and deeply process. They are aware of their own worldview, they are committed to reflective living, and they take control of their own development, not expecting others to do the heavy lifting for them. But they also approach their development with an understanding of how past experiences from their childhood and teen years continue to exert a shaping influence on their worldview in the present. And they recognize the derailers that can stymie their development. Let's capture these ideas in several key principles for active worldview development. In addition, later in the book we'll utilize these same principles as we explore how to immerse your students in environments that readily foster biblical worldview development. People with a maturing biblical worldview will:

1. Understand how their upbringing and past experiences (good, bad, *and* ugly) impact their worldview.
2. Think deeply and regularly about their worldview, frequently asking the following questions:
   - "What do I love, and how have I come to love those things, ideas, goals, and so on?"
   - "What do I think about _____, and why do I think that way?"
   - "What do I do, and why do I do what I do?"
3. Process experiences through reflection, prayer, study, and other disciplines (alone and with friends and mentors), seeking to understand and evaluate them in light of a biblical worldview.
4. Actively seek new experiences with people, places, and ideas that both support and challenge their worldview.
5. Cultivate a lifestyle of balanced and healthful living (emotionally, spiritually, and physically), so there is ample space and time to focus on biblical worldview development.

Notice I called these "principles for *active* worldview development." In thinking about worldview development, you may conclude that you have only two options: develop your worldview intentionally or don't have a worldview. The second option is impossible. I trust by now you are convinced that everyone has a worldview, but not everyone has an intentionally formed, well-organized worldview. I'm assuming, if you've made it this far in this book, you want to have a well-formed worldview as opposed to one with a haphazard jumble of desires, ideas, and behaviors.

Unfortunately, many live life that way, with desires, ideas, and behaviors that contradict one another and are at odds with reality.

Sadly, many Christians live this way. I think we all know Christian friends or family members who set their hearts on earthly things (such as wealth, comfort, and security). They think in ways foreign to Scripture. And they say and do things on a regular basis that are contrary to the kingdom of God. While we all have pockets of our worldview that need ongoing and perhaps radical maturation, some people seem to have no idea how disheveled their worldview really is. They still have a worldview that guides and shapes their desires, thoughts, and actions. It's just not a maturing biblical worldview.

Let's put into operation the principles for active worldview development. Starting with awareness, it begins with asking these questions, "What does your worldview look like? How profoundly is it shaped by the truth of God as revealed in Scripture and in his creation?" When people

> What does your worldview look like? How profoundly is it shaped by the truth of God as revealed in Scripture and in his creation?

first begin to take stock of their worldview, perhaps thinking deeply about it for the first time, it can be unsettling for them. They discover how much of their worldview has been shaped by influences that contradict the truth of Scripture.

Unfortunately, we pick up bad ideas, habits, and influences like we pick up a virus—imperceptibly and without any effort. I find it much easier to catch a cold than to put effort into preventing one. Similarly, a life merely lived at the whim of any desire, idea, or behavior that attracts me is marked by ease. In the long run, though, that easy pathway will have serious consequences, just as an unhealthful diet may be easy for today but have hard future consequences.

If you were to evaluate your physical well-being, you'd start by comparing your health to a standard of what it should be. You'd compare your blood pressure, pulse, weight, and other facets of health to what the experts say are optimal. A similar approach works with evaluating your worldview health.

YOUR WORLDVIEW CHECKUP

Summit Ministries has created an excellent worldview assessment as part of their *Secret Battle of Ideas about God* project. It helps people take the first step in evaluating their worldview and what they believe to be true about the world. I recommend you take Summit's Worldview Checkup as you embark on the journey to understand the contours of your own worldview. While no questionnaire or survey can tell you what your worldview is with 100 percent accuracy, this assessment will give you some idea of what you believe about reality. Additionally, it will sensitize your mind to the kinds of desires, concepts, and ideas that make up a worldview. Thoughtfully completing this assessment can help you to be more aware of your natural, automatic responses to the questions and conundrums in the world around you.

You can find the assessment at secretbattlebook.com/checkup. I encourage you to pause your reading, complete the assessment, and then reflect on your results.[8]

The following are a few questions that can spark quality reflection for you:

- How close were your results to what you expected them to be?

- As you read each of the statements in the assessment, did you identify the answers that you suspected were the "right" ones?
- How would your results compare with how you may have answered the questions ten years ago?
- Where do you perceive you have more work to do in having your worldview shaped by Scripture?

Ideally, this simple exercise helped you be more aware of your worldview. To gain even more value from this experience, compare and contrast your results with a friend or colleague who has also taken the assessment. Ask one another to explain how each of your results reflect what you already knew about yourself and what was a surprise. Share ideas about how to reshape some of your ideas to more accurately reflect a biblical worldview. This exercise of assessing, evaluating, and reflecting on your worldview with a friend is a great example of an experience that energizes and propels worldview development. More on this later.

1. Create a Timeline of Past Influences

Having begun an examination of your worldview by taking the Summit Worldview Checkup, the next thing to do is to reflect on the influences from your past that have shaped your worldview. It would be great if our growing up years were exclusively shaped by Scripture, but even for those of us who grew up in Christian homes, good churches, or even Christian schools, that's just not realistic. The fall of man back in the Garden of Eden impacted every facet of creation, including our upbringing.

I recognize this can be a difficult area to think about. For some, dredging up the past can become overwhelming. Trauma and challenges from childhood and teen years can be painful to recall and can spark all kinds of emotions. Even so, it is helpful to think through how you came to desire, think, and act the way you do. The experiences, relationships, and teachings from your past have played an enormous role in shaping who you are today.

> The experiences, relationships, and teachings from your past have played an enormous role in shaping who you are today.

One effective means of reflecting on the influences from your past is to create a personal worldview development timeline. To begin, brainstorm the key milestones, experiences, and processes from your past that have influenced the formation of your worldview. These can include the following and any other significant experiences:

- your salvation experience
- family influences (such as family faith, church, or religious background, family devotions)
- schools attended
- important mentoring or peer relationships
- worldview classes, books, or resources to which you have been exposed

A helpful aid in creating your timeline can be to talk with people who know you well: a sibling, a longtime friend, or your spouse. They will likely bring up important shaping influences you may have forgotten. My research suggests that even the act of brainstorming out loud with someone else can be formative.

After listing as many of these shaping influences as you can, plot them on a rough timeline of your life from birth until the present. Add as much or as little detail as you wish. Try to categorize them into separate themes, such as family, church (or lack of church), school, peer influences, and so on. Be particularly aware of key mentors in your life and also experiences that disoriented or troubled you. Your goal with this project is to get a big-picture view of the shaping influences that have contributed to your worldview—both positive and negative.

When I talk with others after they've completed this exercise, invariably they report that things come up they never thought about before in relation to their worldview. People also remark that this is a difficult but enjoyable exercise that helps them understand why they desire, think, and act the way they do.

Perhaps now would be a good time to take some pressure off. Don't feel like you need to produce a perfect or comprehensive timeline. The purpose of this is to help facilitate good reflection, not to pinpoint every specific influence you've experienced.

To get the most value out of creating your timeline, I suggest two additional steps after you're confident you've captured a number of significant influences. First, distill into two or three sentences how those influences impacted your current worldview and how you can move closer to a more complete biblical worldview. For instance, a timeline summary statement could read:

> My worldview has been shaped primarily by my irreligious family of origin, my years in public school, my brief exposure to church in my late high school years, and the character coach on my high school football team. It was not until college that my roommate led me to the Lord. I immediately began to consume as much Scripture as possible. My desires, thoughts, and actions

slowly began to change. Now I find myself just beginning to see the battle between the desires, thoughts, and actions promoted in my upbringing and those that are affirmed and encouraged in Scripture.

2. Share Your Timeline with Colleagues

The second step is to share your timeline and your summary statement with friends or, better yet, colleagues at school. Invite them to ask you questions about your timeline. Allow them to inquire about things that are not clear or things about which they are curious. Share more about your milestones than what's on paper. Tell stories about the significant experiences on your timeline, adding details and describing how you think those stories impact you today. Give examples of habitual and natural desires, thoughts, or actions that may be traced directly back to the things you included on your timeline. For bonus points, do this exercise with someone else who also created a timeline, and take turns sharing stories.

If you took the worldview assessment earlier, it can be illuminating to compare your results with your timeline, looking for cause and effect. For instance, your results may show you have a number of ideas that reflect postmodern thinking. Try to make connections between those ideas and the shaping influences from your past. In doing so, you are beginning to see your worldview in a holistic way and to forge new mental connections between the disparate and isolated aspects of your worldview. Bits and pieces can begin to coalesce as you look at them in the larger story of how your worldview has been shaped throughout your lifetime.

After completing the timeline, keep it for future reference. Many leadership and self-development experts suggest pulling away for regular times of reflection and refueling. Your timeline can become an ongoing work that you look at periodically as you reflect on the big picture of your ongoing development. In such times, it can encourage you to keep pursuing development. You may even remember more past influences you can add to your timeline to help make it more complete.

Now that you've taken the time to reflect on your past and how your current worldview has developed, we will take a closer look in the next chapter at those five principles for active worldview development and how they practically play out in your life.

CHAPTER 7

COMMITTING TO
MEANINGFUL
PROCESSING

With a strong foundation of awareness of your worldview and how it has been influenced, you can begin with some new actions that will ideally become habitual. This is where we begin to engage the real engine of worldview development. The processing cycle, including the habitual exposure to new experiences, is followed up by intentionally processing those experiences.

The term *experience* here is used in the broadest sense of the word. An experience is anything that happens to you or that you make happen. It can be anything from doing laundry to reading a blog post to grieving the death of a loved one.

The term *processing* is also used broadly. It means reflecting on an experience to understand it, assign meaning to it, and respond appropriately with affirmed, modified, or new desires, ideas, or actions. If you experience (read) a chapter in a book, you process that experience by thinking about it deeply enough to clearly understand what the author is saying. Then you push deeper to grapple with what the content in the chapter means. Finally, you contemplate how the ideas you read can and will influence your desires, thoughts, or actions. If you experience the loss of a job, you process that through prayer, consultation with trusted friends, and journaling. All these lead to changes in your desires, thoughts, or actions.

> Whether your experience is chosen (watching an online video) or foisted upon you (a car accident you didn't cause), everything can be evaluated, understood, and responded to in light of a biblical worldview. Doing so is the stuff of worldview development.

This cycle is not undirected or isolated. It is squarely situated in the larger context of a commitment to have one's desires, thoughts, and actions more fully align with a biblical worldview. Whether your experience is chosen (watching an online video) or foisted upon you (a car accident you didn't cause), everything can be evaluated, understood, and responded to in light of a biblical worldview. Doing so is the stuff of worldview development.

LOCATING YOUR EXPERIENCES IN THE NARRATIVE FRAMEWORK

In the processing phase, it is critically important to locate your experiences in the narrative framework of *Creation, Fall, Redemption,* and *Restoration* (or *ought, is, can,* and *will*). Imagine reading a novel in which a character experiences loss or grief. You can locate that situation in the *is* part of the biblical narrative. Loss and grief only occur because we live in the context of the fall, our current reality. In assigning meaning to an experience of loss (whether your own or that of someone in a novel or movie), you are exploring one element of the unfortunate way things are. Doing so in the broader context of the biblical narrative keeps you from staying there, recognizing that things *can* and ultimately *will* be different.

The four applied worldview questions from chapter 3 also have a role to play in the processing phase of the cycle. Every experience affords us with the opportunity to ask these questions:

- What's good here that I can *cultivate*?
- What's missing that I can *create*?
- What's evil that I can *curb*?
- What's broken that I can help to *cure*?

These questions can also be applied vicariously, such as in the experiences you observe in a novel or a movie. Even though you can't influence the outcome of a movie or book, you can imagine what you would do if you were in the fictional situation. Or you can evaluate the character's actions and classify them as either the answer to one of the four questions or the opposite. For instance, you can evaluate how a character adds to evil, breaks things or people, scoffs at what is good, or even destroys what has been created.

This is also a great way to evaluate whether a movie is worth watching or a book worth reading. If the characters in the story do these destructive things, and they are celebrated and rewarded, it may not be an appropriate movie or book for entertainment. Worldview analysis—yes. Entertainment—probably not.

Those with a maturing biblical worldview control their own worldview development process and choose specific experiences to provide fodder for processing. There are countless experiences you can choose to engage in for the purpose of worldview development. These experiences should be a mix of those chosen to equip you with knowledge and skills, to expose you to affections that enhance your biblical worldview, and to challenge your worldview.

TAKING CHARGE OF YOUR INFORMATION DIET

Since the term *worldview* emerged on the evangelical scene in the 1970s and 80s, the resources available to support the development of a biblical worldview are virtually limitless. Do you like to interact with new information by reading? There are more biblical worldview books in print than you could read in your lifetime and countless blogs on the subject. Do you learn best by watching a video? YouTube and other online sources are replete with teachings related to worldview. Do you prefer a more immersive experience? Attend one of the many available worldview conferences. The appendix lists quality resources and reputable worldview ministries for you to check out. Consider creating a personalized learning track that will provide ample experience to process as you further develop a biblical worldview.

In that list, you'll also find a number of regular podcasts that can help you. I'm busy just like you, but I have the blessing of time in the car every day, since I live about thirty minutes from the school where I serve. This gives me at least five or six hours a week to leverage for my own worldview development and that of my family. One of my go-to podcasts is the daily *The World and Everything in It*, which is much like National Public Radio, but from a biblical worldview perspective. When I'm with members of my family in the car, we often listen to *World* and press pause to discuss and process what we just heard.

Another podcast I listen to on a regular basis is *BreakPoint* by John Stonestreet from the Colson Center for Biblical Worldview. *BreakPoint* produces five-minute spots that offer commentary on current events from a biblical worldview. They also do weekly half-hour broadcasts that go more in depth into that week's national and world happenings. The input from these sources is great. But again, to maximize their value, you must process the experience. Talk or pray about what you just heard. Think about where the news report fits in the biblical narrative. And consider how you could respond. Can you *cultivate, create, curb,* or *cure* something?

> If you're going to be serious about developing a biblical worldview, you need to create specific input experiences for yourself.

I could devote numerous pages to describing the resources available to you, but space (and likely your attention span) does not allow. The point is, if you're going to be serious about developing a biblical worldview, you need to create specific input experiences for yourself. Then your mind and heart will have plenty of raw material for the all-important processing habit. You have to take charge of your information diet.

STUDYING YOUR BIBLE

Oddly, the next experience we'll discuss is often overlooked in recommendations related to developing a biblical worldview, when it's actually the most important. If you're going to continue growing your biblical worldview, you must be a lifelong reader and student of the Bible. With all the worldview books to read and podcasts to listen to, Scripture itself can be crowded out. I have no intention to be legalistic here. But if you're going to deeply understand the biblical narrative, become an expert in connecting your course content to Scripture, and immerse your students in a biblically rich learning environment, you have no choice but to read and reflect on the Bible every day. The difference, of course, between the Bible and other resources is that it is the ultimate authority on truth. As the writer of Hebrews (in 4:12) teaches us, the Bible is actually living. Each time you pick it up, you are interacting with truth in a way that transcends all other experiences. Read it. Study it. Speak it. Pray it. Live it.

EXPOSING YOURSELF TO OPPOSING IDEAS

Worldview development is supported not only by experiencing resources that are worldview friendly. It's also helpful to be exposed to ideas contrary to a biblical worldview.[9] I teach a worldview class for undergraduate students. In that course, I require them to read selections straight out of the Quran, the *Humanist Manifesto*, Charles Darwin's *The Origin of Species*, and other works. My students are challenged to think deeply about what the proponents of alternate worldviews hold to be true, including finding ideas within them that agree with a biblical worldview.[10]

A similarly helpful prompt for developing a biblical worldview is to interact with people who do not share your worldview. This can be anything from an isolated grocery store conversation to a service project in a different part of town or a meaningful friendship with a neighbor. Getting to know people who do not share your worldview can be challenging to your assumptions, your patience, and even to your political loyalties. The emerging adults in my research project consistently talked about how being friends with non-Christians and reflecting on those friendships was a key part of affirming and nurturing deep commitment to their own worldview.

LIVING A WORLDVIEW DEVELOPMENT LIFESTYLE

I feel like I may be overwhelming you at this point. You may be thinking, "Yeah, right, Roger! I'm a busy high school math teacher. You're telling me I have to listen to podcasts, be a Bible scholar, and now I have to add *The Origin of Species* to my reading list and make friends with all my non-Christian neighbors?" Please don't check out on me here. Remember what Bruce Lockerbie said? Developing a biblical worldview is the most important thing you can do to become a teacher who immerses students in an environment that fulfills the promise of being a distinctively different kind of school. It's hard work and takes enormous effort, but it's essential to our calling and purpose.

Also, it's not necessary to make up for lost time all in one month or year. The suggestions I'm making are lifelong habits. Over time, as you continue to see all of life filled with worldview development opportunities, you will incrementally build a habit of regular processing. This will come more naturally to you, to the point where worldview development is a conscious lifestyle. We learned from the emerging adults in my research project that any experience can be leveraged for worldview development. This happens if you are aware of the opportunities to do so and are committed to meaningful processing.

IDENTIFYING DERAILERS

We should not neglect the final element of the worldview development model we are using as the basis for our suggestions. You'll remember from chapter 5 that there are threats to intentional worldview development—derailers that can seriously upend the worldview development process. Distractions, stress, apathy, and trials can all gang up on us to crowd out working on our worldview.

We usually think of these as threats to our students, but what about us as adults? If we're not careful and aware, we can certainly fall victim to them as well.

1. Distractions

Social media is not just for the kids anymore. I can remember when Facebook first became popular with teens and young adults around 2007 and 2008. When Mom and Dad, Grandma and Grandpa found out they could join the fun, the younger set left in droves, and we were left with a huge distraction. It can happen to all of us. When I sat down to write this evening, I was distracted by my newsfeed (which seems to be made up of only 10 percent of stuff I want to see anyway). We can get caught up with all kinds of online distractions: online idea boards for clever book report ideas; March Madness; or endless cycles of news and commentary. If we develop a biblical worldview, we will need to be self-disciplined with even the good and appropriate things that distract us, choosing instead to invest our time and attention in more worthy experiences.

> Find a place to deposit your cell phone when you get home, making a conscious decision to go to it when necessary as opposed to storing it at the ready in your pocket.

I have two specific suggestions for managing the distraction machine you likely carry with you everywhere you go—your smartphone. If we're not attentive, we can become just like the teens we see at the bus stop with hunched necks, glowing faces, and no connection to the human beings standing right next to them. First, find a place to deposit your cell phone when you get home, making a conscious decision to go to it when necessary as opposed to storing it at the ready in your pocket. There was a time when we had to get up to get the information and communication we needed. Our phones only reached as far as that spiral cord would allow. Kitchens full of family members often resembled limbo dances or double-dutch jump rope as we navigated the cord. We can survive without our phones in our pocket.

In addition, putting some distance between you and your phone can actually help with worldview development in a more direct way. My family and I have identified one way the Gutenberg-to-Google revolution had been robbing us of valuable worldview development exercises. Dinner times have always offered my wife, five kids, and me many opportunities to have significant discussions. We talk about current events, biblical texts, apologetics, and many other topics. The discussions we have are rich and are a key part of our worldview development. Each of us, however, carry a universe of information in our pockets. When we would have discussions and hit upon some fact or information about which we were unsure, we would pull out our phones and race to see who could find the answer first. It resembled the Bible sword drills of the past.

Over time, it dawned on us what was happening. We were becoming intellectually and collaboratively lazy. We'd jump right to the answer by doing an internet search instead of jointly trying to remember a fact, a quote from a movie, or a line of thinking on a subject. This was short-circuiting the processes of developing intellectual persistence and working together with a communal train of thought, helping us arrive at the answer or idea that we needed. In so doing, we wasted many opportunities for quality processing. While instant answers may make your conversations more efficient, they rob you of the precious exercise of pushing through foggy thinking to clarity in community with others.

The second suggestion I have is to change your behavior with a simple play on words. Not only will this solution help with the distraction issue, it will harness your management of distractions for direct worldview development. As I mentioned before, I can easily get caught up in scrolling through social media to see what's new and interesting. It may be just a few moments of scrolling, or I can wake from the scrolling stupor and realize I just wasted ten or fifteen minutes or more.

It's a happy coincidence that someone decided to call that repetitive swipe of the finger scrolling. Think for a moment about that word. Do you see something there that can prompt your brain to do something more productive with the blocks of minutes you sometimes waste on social media? While what I'm about to say may sound cheesy, sometimes we humans need to see something in a new way to trigger us to opt for more healthy behaviors. The root for the word *scrolling* is a word that should remind us to pick up the Bible and read. Got it yet?

> When you're tempted to scroll through social media, you can be prompted to pick up your modern-day "scroll" and read the Bible. You likely have several Bibles in your home and can strategically place them in the locations where you may be tempted to consume social media.

You already know that ancient people of faith didn't have ready access to neatly bound books like we do. They had scrolls, or at least they had access to such scrolls through their spiritual community. With this in mind, when you're tempted to scroll through social media, you can be prompted to pick up your modern-day "scroll" and read the Bible. You likely have several Bibles in your home and can strategically place them in the locations where you may be tempted to consume social media. Instead of electronic scrolling, do some "scrolling" with the Word of God. Wouldn't it be great to develop a new habit of consuming snippets of Scripture on a regular basis throughout the day, instead of logging minutes or hours of pointless screen time?

2. Stress

Stress is another derailer and is a huge issue for teachers. The demands on a teachers' time and the challenges that today's students can bring to the classroom seem to increase each year. I was at a major Christian school conference recently where an entire learning track was devoted to protecting and fostering teachers' emotional well-being in the midst of one of the most demanding jobs on the planet. Your ability to effectively process life experiences and fold them into your overall growth is inversely related to your stress level. Unchecked stress is the quintessential interloper, moving in on the spiritual and mental space you need to live a reflective life. If you find stress consuming more and more space in your life, you may need to say no to some worthwhile activities. Additionally, you may need to implement some new commitments to promote your emotional and spiritual health, such as solitude, silence, fasting, and other spiritual disciplines.

3. Apathy

Since you're a Christian educator, apathy likely has little place in your life. It's hard to get up in the morning to face a long day of the ups and downs of working with students if you're apathetic. However, trials and challenges abound, and as a teacher you're probably well acquainted with those. Just like the emerging adults in my research project, difficulties have a way of either pushing you toward or away from worldview development. The difference is in how you respond to those challenges.

4. Trials

Embracing difficulty with a heart to learn and situating your trials in the biblical narrative can further develop your worldview. Ignoring hard things and disengaging from trials will only serve to numb you to the work God wants to do in you and will ultimately stall your worldview development. Or worse yet, doing so may encourage a nonbiblical view of trials to capture your affections.

MODELING BIBLICAL WORLDVIEW IMMERSION

Efforts expended in developing your own worldview will certainly bear good fruit in your teaching. It makes sense that, if your aim is to immerse your students in a worldview-rich environment, you need to be growing in your own worldview. You can't provide for others what you don't have yourself. But there's another reason to actively develop your biblical worldview, and this will link the ideas in this chapter with the ideas in the chapters to come.

Research repeatedly demonstrates that modeling is an important facet of shaping students, and this logically extends to shaping students' worldviews. Some experts would even go so far as to say that what teachers live out in front

> What teachers live out in front of their students is even more important than the content he or she teaches.

of their students is even more important than the content he or she teaches. As Nicholas Wolterstorff (1980, p. 62) said, "It looks as if there is in humanity a tendency to imitate those who are loved or esteemed." As Jesus said in Luke 6:40, the fully trained student will be *like his teacher*. If you're committed to actively developing your own worldview and you share that journey with your students, you've taken the first step in providing a biblical worldview immersion experience for those who call you "teacher."

PART 2

CREATING A BIBLICAL
WORLDVIEW IMMERSIVE
ENVIRONMENT

INTRODUCTION

Creating biblical worldview immersive environments starts with teachers who are actively developing their own worldview. But it certainly doesn't end there. Building on the foundation of your own growth and discovery, you go on to create an environment for your students. It's like building and setting up a greenhouse where conditions are ideal for worldview development. Remember, this isn't merely about teaching the tenets of a biblical worldview, though that is definitely a part of the process. This is about an immersive experience in every subject area. Everything in your relationship with your students, the content you teach, and the learning activities you plan are focused on the knowledge, behaviors, and inclinations they will need for a lifetime of intentional worldview development. Similar to the *pedagogium* of the Middle Ages, you invite students into a way of living and being that immerses them in a reality shaped and defined by a biblical worldview.

What I'm going to outline in part 2 is based on a simple idea. Rather than a random series of strategies, classroom activities, or even full courses that we *think* may help our students gain a biblical worldview, we should develop strategies based on the data from real research. There's plenty of room to do more research on how worldviews develop, and I hope some aspiring researchers reading this book will do it! However, we do have a good idea of how a biblical worldview develops in the kind of young adults we hope to graduate from our schools. With this data in hand, we can work backward through the years of schooling to build the skills, desires, and knowledge the research suggests our students will need.

FOUR CENTRAL TEACHING COMMITMENTS

So here's the bottom-line idea we'll unpack in this section. To help our students develop a biblical worldview, we need to create and sustain a classroom environment fueled by four central teaching commitments:

1. Practical guidance toward desiring the kingdom of God, including:
   - establishing habits that can lead to this desire
   - introduction to godly role models, including live role models and those in literature, movies, and history
   - interactions with individuals who do not embrace a biblical worldview
2. Age-appropriate practice in the reflective disciplines that enable students to effectively process their experiences
3. Engaging learning experiences, as opposed to teaching methods that encourage students to passively receive content
4. Subject-based experience with the truth claims and practical application of a biblical worldview

I should note here that there's *much* more a school can

do to help students develop a biblical worldview. In this section, I've devoted a chapter to school leaders to explain their responsibility to structure the entire student experience with your school toward a focus on biblical world-view development. The classroom is critical, but it's not everything, and your students' worldview development does not rest on your shoulders alone. In fact, if you're reading this book individually, I recommend you buy a copy for the head of your school. Your efforts to create an immersive worldview experience in your classroom will be greatly enhanced if your leaders focus your entire school community on worldview development.

> The classroom is critical, but it's not everything, and your students' worldview development does not rest on your shoulders alone.

WHAT YOU WON'T FIND

Before we begin part 2, I need to offer an important disclaimer. I'm not sure what you're expecting in the next several chapters. What you *won't* find is a completely new set of teaching strategies that no one has ever thought of before. As Solomon wrote over three thousand years ago, there's nothing new under the sun (Ecclesiastes 1:9), and that includes the classroom. Biblical worldview immersion is not accomplished with novel pedagogies. It happens when we approach our classrooms more holistically and infuse new purpose into the teaching and learning strategies we use. We select those strategies based on a well-thought-out framework for how students develop a biblical worldview.

Your success in creating the kind of *pedagogium* we've been describing will not necessarily come from devising brand-new pedagogies. As David Smith says, "There is no straight path from Bible verses to pedagogical choices" (2018, p. 37). While there are many fantastic learning methods exemplified in Scripture, you can't necessarily point to chapter and verse for every method you choose to include in your lesson plans.

Let's think about how a biblical worldview should shape our view of learning methods by looking at reading as an example. Reading is a complex activity requiring several different processes to occur virtually simultaneously. Seeing, recognizing symbols as letters, phonetic decoding, processing, discerning meaning, and emotional response all come together in a moment as a person takes in information through the learning method of reading. We often classify the activity I described as neutral, as it's neither Christian nor non-Christian—it's just reading. But is this an accurate way to look at one of the most awe-inspiring capabilities of human beings?

Let's go back to one of the bedrock foundations of a biblical worldview. This gives insight into how to view reading, math operations, the microscope, or any one of thousands of ways that we learn. It also explains the ways we use what we learn and the ways we steward the aspects of reality over which we as humans have authority.

What would life be like if there had been no fall of man? We'd still be reading, discovering, using microscopes, thinking, leveraging what we learn, and sharing our knowledge and skills with others. In short, we'd be doing many of the same things we've come to understand as neutral, just without the shattering impact of the fall. Children would still need to master phonics. But they'd be able to do so without having a bad attitude, without giving up when it gets hard, and without the possibility of discovering the negative and sinful things waiting to be consumed by their eyes.

In light of this, to look at teaching methods as Christian or non-Christian is a false classification. It can actually promote a view of learning inconsistent with one of the core principles of a biblical worldview, namely Kuyper's declaration, "There is not a square inch in the whole domain of our human existence over which Christ, who is Sovereign over all, does not cry: 'Mine!'" A better, more thoughtful, and nuanced approach to learning methods would be to say that, in a general sense, everything legitimately enabling human beings to learn (as we were designed to do) is indeed kingdom learning.

> To look at teaching methods as Christian or non-Christian is a false classification. It can actually promote a view of learning inconsistent with one of the core principles of a biblical worldview.

Others who hold to substitute worldviews also use many of these same learning strategies as well. They may have even used them first, before we ever thought to do so. But, when we use them, we're not stealing ideas from them, we're just implementing what already belongs to Christ. This should guard against the misguided expectation that a whole new set of learning methods can be classified as Christian, just waiting to be unearthed and implemented so we can produce amazing young adults in our schools.

Conversely, some practices Christian teachers regularly do can work against the way God has made us. Teachers who put minimal effort into getting to know their students individually ignore the deeply relational nature of human beings, which reflects God's trinitarian nature. When teachers fail to give students opportunities to apply what they're learning in real-world situations, they may be inadvertently supporting a "hearing but not doing" (James 1:22) posture toward life. If teachers exhibit no joy in teaching, mechanically going through the motions of getting content across to their students, they set up major barriers to learning. Teachers who rely exclusively on lecture disregard the reality that God has made his students to be responsive, active agents in their environments. These examples may seem extreme, but I've seen permutations of all of them in various degrees throughout my time in Christian education. These all demonstrate teaching practices that could be considered non-Christian because they are out of sync with how God has made human beings.

SEE, ENGAGE, AND RESHAPE

Taking a cue from David Smith (2018), I want to set up the second section of the book by challenging us with three simple words that help us infuse a kingdom way into our teaching: *see, engage*, and *reshape*. *See* prods us to think about all we do with our students, driven by the question, "What if we took a fresh look at each of our teaching practices and wondered whether they really resonated with the kingdom of God?" (Smith, 2018, p. 70).

Engage reminds us that, whenever we have a choice about what teaching strategy to use, by default we ought to go with the one (or ones) that promote maximal cognitive, emotional, and physical engagement with the subject matter and each other.

Finally, *reshape* refers to the reflective habit of evaluating and refining *how* we teach, with a deep conviction that meaning, purpose, and ideals are conveyed not only in *what* we communicate, but in *how* we communicate as well. Our "gestures, postures, images, resources, rhythms, silences, pauses, repetitions, omissions, room layouts, and more" (Smith, 2018, p. 73) are all raw materials we can harness to craft the unique kingdom learning environment (*pedagogium*) we are after. Instead of blindly doing what we've always done, we can, with full awareness, choose to incrementally reshape our teaching to more faithfully reflect the process whereby human beings can develop a truly biblical worldview.

Smith reminds us, "We tend to perpetuate patterns of practice for reasons that have little to do with clear-eyed commitment to the convictions that shaped them or cast-iron evidence that they are valuable" (2018, p. 70). Some parents unthinkingly parent the way they were parented. Athletic coaches often uncritically coach the way they were coached. For teachers, it's all too easy to settle on the familiar, regardless of whether or not we have come to a settled decision that that is the most effective way to operate.

After experiencing and processing this book, you will likely employ some of the same teaching strategies you currently use, and you may pick up a few new ones as well. But the strategies must be fueled by the heart and purpose behind them and the aims you're looking to accomplish. And even if you do use some of the same strategies you've always used, my prayer is that they will be infused with new kingdom life as you submit them to Christ's rulership over your classroom and the hearts and minds of your students.

> Fix in your imagination a vision of the kind of home you want to create for your students. Imagine them signing up to "live" with you for a time in a place specifically designed for them.

As you move into these next several chapters, please fix in your imagination a vision of the kind of home you want to create for your students. Imagine them signing up to "live" with you for a time in a place specifically designed for them. It will be a place where they will taste and see that the Lord is good (Psalm 34:8), that his rulership over all creation is a good thing, and that it really works. As Professor Smith would say, when you plan your teaching, you're not just creating lesson plans. You're designing a home for your students where you can "live together for a while, a place to which students are welcomed as guests and in which they can grow" (Smith, 2018, p. 12).

CHAPTER 8

SHAPING THE HEART'S DESIRES

Most teacher resources on biblical worldview start with content. You'll remember from earlier discussions that content is important—really important—but it's not everything. Obviously, we need to clearly articulate the truths of a biblical worldview to our students, and there is benefit in reciting them when they are asked. I don't, however, believe this is the best place to start when thinking about a distinctively Christian approach to teaching.

Actually, if we start with content, there won't be much challenge in that. Let's face it—we educators are great at transferring content. Sure, we have to do some heavy lifting at times to understand and then repackage content in a way that our students will grasp. But generally, we tend to excel at this, and talking to (or at) our students comes quite naturally. Shaping desires, however, is a whole other thing, and quite an intimidating thing at that. But it is possible and, for Christian teachers in Christian schools, it is the heart (pun intended) of what we're trying to do.

But how does a teacher intentionally shape students' desires such that they develop a heart inclination toward the kingdom of God and his rulership in every area of life? This is the essential core desire of one who has a biblical worldview. How do you shape any desire in someone else for that matter?

USING HABITS TO SHAPE DESIRES

One of my all-time favorite parenting moments was with my son, Andrew, in the eighth grade. It was the time of year to choose a musical composition for him to play on his baritone horn in the solo adjudication at our state music festival. Each year, we'd go online to find the list of approved works. Then we went to YouTube to listen to them and find one that we thought would work. This particular year, I remember sitting on my bed and scrolling through option after option, listening to some really great music together.

After sampling several potential pieces, we found Bach's Minuet in G, from "Anna Magdalena Bach Notebook." It's a complex, beautiful composition, and we were both thinking it would be a good fit for Andrew. Picture the scene—a dad and his eighth-grade son listening to classical music together. But it gets better . . . after taking in the minuet, Andrew threw himself back on the bed and breathlessly confessed, "Dad, this is *so* beautiful!" Though I was glad we found a piece of music he'd be motivated to master for the festival, I was even more struck by the fact that classical music could so captivate my son. Of course, I didn't make a big deal about it at the time, not wanting to seem like anything was out of the ordinary and risk spoiling the moment. The more I reflected on the experience, though, I realized Andrew was expressing an inclination toward a beautiful piece of music. And that that didn't just happen. It was the result of repeated, engaging, and celebrated exposure to that genre of music.

Over my kids' childhood, I've exposed them to all kinds of music, including classical music, which most children—especially middle schoolers—tend to avoid like broccoli or lima beans. But from our children's earliest years, we listened to many different genres of music at home and in the car, including classical. Sometimes it would be Toby Mac or 1970s Imperials. Other times, we'd break out "Beethoven's Wig" or other children's adaptations of classical works. Sometimes the kids would choose the tunes; sometimes my wife, Lori, and I were in charge. Even today, when most of my kids are now young adults, they all get quiet when "Gabriel's Oboe" finds its way into my playlist.

No matter the type of music we'd play, we always commented on what we liked (or not) about it. We'd dissect the lyrics or listen for the different instruments' parts and then *ooh and ah* over the really complicated or genuinely novel sections. Music appreciation was, and still is, one of our family pastimes. The result of consistent, engaging, and celebrated exposure to music has been to shape what my children like and want. This is a super-practical example of the truth of Proverbs 29:17: "Train up a child in the way he should go, and when he is old, he will not depart from it." This proverb has more to do with shaping desires through the habits of childhood than it is a parenting guarantee.

As this simple example demonstrates, desires can be shaped. One of the chief ways of doing so is by exposing children to the thing or concept that we want them to desire. Mere exposure, though, is only the beginning. The exposure should be consistent over a long period of time and should be actively engaged and overtly celebrated. It's not enough to have classical music playing in the background of life like a soundtrack. We need to engage the music through discussion, evaluation, and even imitation. Perhaps most importantly, we need to joyfully celebrate the music. If you can't personally identify with an inclination toward music, perhaps you can substitute baseball, hunting, cooking, or some other worthy desire. The point is that children's desires can be shaped. Teachers are not relegated to sitting on the sidelines biting our nails while our students cultivate and express their own innate desires.

> The exposure should be consistent over a long period of time and should be actively engaged and overtly celebrated.

James K. A. Smith has written extensively about this truth in his book *Desiring the Kingdom* (2009). His major premise is that human beings are first and foremost *desiring* beings, as opposed to *thinking* beings. As teachers, we ought to carefully evaluate our assumptions about educating such beings to see if indeed we are honoring the way they really are. Smith rightly suggests, "Education is a wholistic endeavor that includes the whole person . . . in a process of formation that aims our desires" (p. 39). He goes on to state, "We are what we love, and our love is shaped, primed, and aimed by liturgical practices that take hold of our gut and aim our heart to certain ends" (p. 40).

By liturgical practices, he's not only referring to church routines for worship services, though those would apply here as well. He uses that term to mean specific and intentional habits that, when consistently practiced over time, shape a person's desires. These habits naturally create desires without necessarily arriving at a logical, well-considered decision to want them. Habits (consistently practiced actions or activities) are to the heart what regular shortcuts across a lawn are to a yard. They both create well-worn pathways that can be seen and used repeatedly.

If we return to Andrew's unsolicited expression of appreciation (desire) for Bach's Minuet in G, we can see how the habits that were part of his childhood resulted in a specific inclination. This is a great starting place for thinking about the sorts of habits we want to create for our students—habits that can lead to desires consistent with a biblical worldview. Let's consider just one classroom habit that can help to aim a student's desires toward elements of the kingdom of God and what is good and right.

UTILIZING COMMON CLASSROOM ROUTINES

Reading groups are a feature of most elementary classrooms. This exposes students to books they might not have the stamina to read by themselves. It stretches them beyond their own reading level by reading with peers and with their teacher close by as a coach and guide. However, when a teacher understands an immersive biblical worldview environment, she can also leverage group reading time to help shape their desires in ways that are consistent with a biblical worldview.

I once heard of a master teacher using a somewhat challenging book, *The Door in the Wall*, by Marguerite de Angeli, for a fourth-grade reading group. The book is above this reading level, and the material and themes are significantly more meaningful and worthwhile than many other popular books for this age. Still, this teacher felt it would be good to stretch her students with something a bit more demanding, knowing great worldview treasures could be found in the book.

At the start, the students had a hard time understanding the language of the book and struggled to keep interested. The teacher pressed on day after day, sometimes having the students read and at other times reading aloud to them. By the end of the book, the students hung on every word, excitedly *loving* (or desiring) it and wondering how the conflicts masterfully woven by the author would be resolved. The main theme of *The Door in the Wall* is a key biblical worldview lesson. When everything seems lost and every option leads to a dead-end wall, God can still providentially open doors that can lead to joy and fruitful service. Pretty deep stuff

> She did all of this in a winsome, joyful manner, creating an environment that captured the students' hearts and helped them experience the joy of great literature for themselves.

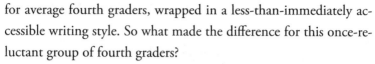

for average fourth graders, wrapped in a less-than-immediately accessible writing style. So what made the difference for this once-reluctant group of fourth graders?

One obvious element of this teacher's success with her students was that she didn't give up. Instead, day by day, reading group by reading group, she persevered in the habit of reading quality, worldview-rich literature. But just as important as her perseverance, the way in which she read with her students held the key to the shaping of their desires. As they read each chapter, the teacher would often stop to discuss the content and draw the students' attention to interesting, entertaining usages of words, to significant ideas, and to biblical themes. And she did all of this in a winsome, joyful manner, creating an environment that captured the students' hearts and helped them experience the joy of great literature for themselves. I'm smiling as I picture several fourth graders sitting in a circle, hungry to keep flipping pages to find out what happens next in a book that most fourth graders would never choose to read on their own.

You may be thinking, "Every elementary teacher does reading groups. What's so different about that?" You're right, reading groups are standard operating procedures for elementary classes. What's different is the intentionality with which the teacher harnessed a common teaching approach in service of incremental worldview development. She selected a book rich in biblical worldview themes. She stretched her students with a book they wouldn't choose to read. She was attentive to the worldview-shaping moments the book created. And she modeled the kind of desires she wanted her students to develop. In short, she was providing her students with a repeated learning moment that not only engaged their reading skills but their hearts as well. James K. A. Smith would call this intentional, sustained reading-group habit a *classroom liturgy* that has the power to shape desire.

Classroom habits for shaping desires consistent with a biblical worldview can be just about anything a teacher intentionally plans and expects students to do on a regular basis. They can be less involved and intense than a month-long reading group. Of course, the habits should have as their aim inculcating a desire consistent with a biblical worldview. Mere classroom routines common in all classrooms are not enough to shape kingdom desires. However, it doesn't take much for a habit to become part of the constellation of experiences that point toward good and right desires. Ideally, every teacher and coach in the school puts effort into crafting expectations around habits that can appropriately shape biblically consistent desires—from *wanting* to treat others well to *wanting* to be involved in God's grand work of redemption of all things.

NURTURING DESIRES THROUGH CONSISTENCY

Left on their own, students will not want to do what is right, and creating habits of goodness trains them in thought and behavioral patterns. As those patterns take root, they begin to realign desires. This is consistent with the famous maxim, "We are what we repeatedly do" (often attributed to Aristotle, but actually written by Will Durant).

> The things you choose to prize and to which you commit yourself bend your heart in their direction.

Think about how this works with healthy food. If you train yourself to consistently eat what is good, and you celebrate your culinary and self-discipline victories along the way, eventually your desires will bend toward that which you have been practicing. You probably have examples in your own life where your desires changed to conform to your habits. This principle reflects Jesus's words in Matthew 6:21 when he affirmed the "law of treasuring" by stating, "Where your treasure is, there your heart will be also." The things you choose to prize and to which you commit yourself bend your heart in their direction. Here are a few additional simple examples of how this can be applied in the classroom as part of an overall immersive biblical worldview experience.

A math teacher can require students to greet at least three other students by name and with a firm handshake at the start of every class, inculcating a sense of honoring and valuing others. A science teacher can start every Friday's class highlighting a particular scientist from history and how he or she *created, cultivated, cured,* or *curbed* using science. To close the discussion, the teacher can require the students to salute the scientist to affirm his or her work.

I hesitate to keep giving you specific examples here, because I don't want this book to become a resource of tips and tricks. I want to provide just enough illustrations to spur you to think of habits that you can implement in your classroom. These habits that can be a part of shaping the desires of your students so they will ultimately desire the kingdom of God above all else—the foundation of a biblical worldview. Remember, for habits to be effective in nurturing desires consistent with a biblical worldview, they must be consistent, engaging, and constantly celebrated.

MODELING

As I reflect on my Christian school teenage years, I can readily identify several key mentors who took special interest in me and held me to high standards. At the time, I didn't necessarily appreciate them. But now, whenever I have the opportunity, I like to tell their stories to honor their investment in my life. Even though their impact was not readily apparent in my desires and actions, over time their investment earned significant compounding interest, and the dividends are still paying out. Mr. Jansson, Mr. Rittenger, and Mr. Barfield—all teachers at my Christian school on Long Island—mentored me by modeling various facets of a biblical worldview for me. They each ultimately became part of God's design to shape my desires for the

> Young people will adapt their behaviors and even adopt brand new behaviors after observing how their mentors live their lives.

kingdom. Mr. Jansson modeled mercy and patience with a hard-nosed younger version of me. Mr. Rittenger modeled an absolute confidence in the power of truth. And Mr. Barfield modeled and required serious commitment. All three lived out Augustine's counsel to "attract them by your way of life if you want them to receive . . . teaching from you" (Leinenweber, 1992, p. 99).

It's not hard to see how modeling aspects of desires that are consistent with a biblical worldview for our students can impact their desire to develop a biblical worldview for themselves. I suppose it is hardly worth noting the obvious here, and we covered this in a previous chapter when we talked about developing our own worldview as teachers; but if you're not actively developing a biblical worldview and overtly modeling the desires, thoughts, and behaviors that reflect Christ's redemptive work in and through your life, you're missing the boat completely. This is called a "nonstarter" for the Christian schoolteacher. I assume that you are actively developing your own worldview and that you want to demonstrate it for your students. So why is modeling so important when it comes to shaping desires?

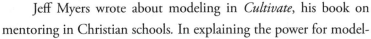

Jeff Myers wrote about modeling in *Cultivate*, his book on mentoring in Christian schools. In explaining the power for modeling, he cited research that suggests young people will adapt their behaviors and even adopt brand new behaviors after observing how their mentors live their lives. When a trusted adult demonstrates good desires, students are drawn to change their own desires to match their mentors (Myers, 2010). As I said earlier, the changes may not be readily apparent—that's okay. Trust the process and, more importantly, the God behind the process, and continue modeling.

> Role models (live or represented in media) who choose what is good and right can help to shape good and right desires and ideals in students.

More than live modeling, though, students are impacted by the representations of individuals desiring what is good and right (or not) in literature and movies and other forms of media (Wolterstorff, 1980, p. 51). Wolterstorff says that Plato himself advocated the elimination of all literature that portrayed humans or the gods doing what they should not be doing. I think we all understand this intuitively; what students read and see in various forms of media shapes their desires. If students are consistently presented with media role models who desire what is not good and ultimately act on those desires, they will likely develop similar desires. The opposite is also true; role models (live or represented in media) who choose what is good and right can help to shape good and right desires and ideals in students.

I'll talk about this subject more in depth in the chapter addressed to Christian school leaders. But here is a great place to mention the enormous importance of carefully choosing the materials you use with your students. I know that, generally speaking, you follow a set instructional plan or curriculum provided by your school. However, I also know that classroom teachers have a significant degree of freedom when it comes to the ancillary materials they use with their students. Given the power of modeling, I urge you to find media (books, movies, and other materials) to use with your students that portray characters making wise and good choices.

I often hear from teachers that they feel it's important to expose their students to all kinds of characters so that their students can see the depravity of the world and the consequences of sinful choices. I do agree that this is important and we should not shelter our students from wisely guided exposure to depravity. Students certainly need to see people making poor choices and to be led to understand how those poor choices impact the characters and those around them. However, in my experience, many experienced Christian schoolteachers seem to think that is a *primary* goal as they choose materials for their classes.

I don't think any student today comes to school lacking exposure to depravity. It's inescapable, from billboards to taxi-cab roof placards, from Netflix to Instagram and Hollywood movies and even their own home situations. Exposure to depravity is pretty much the norm for our students. What's *not* normal is exposure to books and movies in which characters make wise choices and in which the results of those choices mirror the principles of the kingdom of God.

This counsel is not only for the language arts teachers reading this book—it is actually for all teachers. You may, as a science or math teacher, be thinking that this concept of vicarious modeling is not applicable to you, since you don't read fiction or show movie clips in your class. But if you're going to create for your students an immersive worldview experience, you may want to consider doing so. I'm not suggesting that you convert your units on atoms or qua-dratic formulas into literature studies. However, even in science or math, you can benefit from looking at role models who are living out a biblical worldview.

One of the most brilliant people I've ever had the privilege of knowing is Dr. Raymond Damadian. He's a research medical doctor who invented the magnetic resonance imaging machine (MRI) and a strong, faithful Christian. Over lunch one day, he explained to me the science of the MRI and the process he used to develop the technology that has literally changed the medical world. He truly *created* something that was missing.

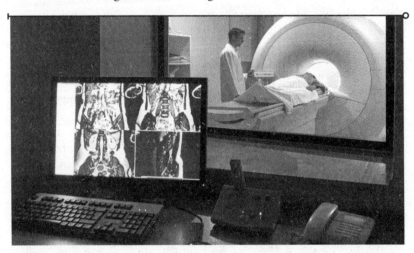

I'd like to say I kept up with his explanations, but he was way out of my league. However, when I heard the compelling way he described his invention, and knowing he was a committed Christian, I knew I had to get him to our school to share his story with our students.

This was so important that we interrupted an entire afternoon of classes for an all-high-school assembly. Dr. Damadian gave an amazing presentation on the development of the MRI. We also invited parents and any STEM-interested friends of the school. The assembly hall was packed with curious students of science, adults and students alike. Of course, the scientific content was phenomenal, and Dr. Damadian did not disappoint on that count. But perhaps even more germane to our discussion here, he radiated a winsome commitment to probing and shaping elements of God's creation for the benefit of human flourishing. He was a living example of leveraging absolutely brilliant science to live out a biblical worldview. Yes, our students missed a few classes that day. But being exposed to a giant of an inventor who modeled good and right desires was well worth the missed class time.

Another great example of a person whom you can invite into your science classroom through a book or movie is Dr. Ben Carson, famed neurosurgeon and outspoken Christian. His book *Gifted Hands* was later made into a movie of the same name. It documents his transformation from troubled youth to a towering intellect, not neglecting to clearly portray his reliance on the wisdom that comes from God. In one particularly poignant movie scene, Dr. Carson labors over how to perform an extremely delicate and dangerous twenty-four-hour surgery to separate conjoined twins. As he ponders the ominous challenge, he sits at home late at night poring over medical books and his own legal pad chock full of notes and ideas—the stuff of real science.

But he's also shown praying about the problem, seeking God for a solution. Over the course of several hours, a surgical strategy dawns on him, and it's clear the strategy came from the Lord. This is precisely what our students need to see—people who are fully reliant on God's wisdom to effectively use their talents and training to *create, cultivate, cure,* and *curb.* Time spent in exposing our students to these kinds of role models is never wasted. For some reason, we don't normally think of taking the time for this kind of exposure for our students in math and science. I hope you can see how marrying your course content to biblical worldview modeling can help to shape your students' desires.

You may not have a Dr. Damadian in your hometown like I did. However, if you spread out your net, you'll find folks in the sciences who are living out a biblical worldview in the midst of many vocations who have great stories to tell. Your students need to meet and interact with role models of this sort. Their desires will be shaped and their learning in class will be formed into a vision for their own future—a vision shaped by a desire to extend the kingdom of God through their vocation.

I picked science as the subject of these few examples since we tend to not naturally think about books, movies, or guests in courses like science or math. Certainly, if we can find worthy individuals to set up as role models in these fields, it should not be hard to think of ideas for doing so in language arts or history classes. If you're not inviting biblically faithful role models into your classrooms, you're missing an important way to bend the desires of your students toward a biblical worldview.

EXPOSING STUDENTS TO PEOPLE OF OTHER WORLDVIEWS

The young adults in my study also identified another way in which they were motivated to pursue a biblical worldview. Repeatedly, study participants told me about how exposure to people who did *not* share a biblical worldview motivated them to explore and refine their own worldview in greater depth. At first pass, it may sound like a contradiction to the last few chapters. But in getting to know the stories of people who didn't agree with them, they were all the more resolute in developing their own worldview.

I've experienced this same dynamic many times. It's happened as I've heard musings on life by a secular neighbor, attended lectures by non-Christian professors and political candidates, or watched grieving Hindus on the banks of the Ganges River push their deceased loved one out from shore on a funeral pyre. When I'm exposed to people who are living life outside a biblical worldview, I'm always prompted to reflect on why people believe and live the way they do. And as a consequence, I find myself desiring to further refine my own worldview.

> When I'm exposed to people who are living life outside a biblical worldview, I'm always prompted to reflect on why people believe and live the way they do. And as a consequence, I find myself desiring to further refine my own worldview.

I'm not suggesting here that you throw your students into the deep end of secularism with no life vest. I'm also not suggesting you challenge your third-grade class with a presentation by a postmodern author. But short of these drastic and unwise moves, you can carefully expose your students to people who do not share a biblical worldview.

One way to do this is through literature. It is valuable to read books that demonstrate to your students the tragic consequences of living at odds with a biblical worldview. This is a way to "meet" and interact with people who don't think and act like you do. To do so effectively, you will need to prepare your students well beforehand and be ready to process what you are reading with your students along the way. When deciding what literature to use with your students, it's helpful to keep in mind a simple four-word evaluation tool I picked up from Oliver DeMille in his book *A Thomas Jefferson Education* (2000).

DeMille classifies a piece of literature's treatment of life themes as one of four options: *whole, broken, bent,* or *healing. Whole* literature demonstrates a life lived consistent with kingdom principles. While it may be fraught with difficulties, it is the truly good life—the life to be desired. Wise choices are prized and celebrated, and readers can get caught up in seeing life work out the way God designed. *Broken* stories show the tragic consequences of unwise living, casting them as clearly undesirable. They don't sanitize sin or living outside of a biblical worldview, but they don't celebrate it either. *Bent* books put sin and anti-God themes on display, but they celebrate the sin, not showing its deceptive nature and ugly results. Finally, *healing* books are most often either *whole* or *broken* books in which the reader is "profoundly moved, changed, or significantly improved by his reading experience" (DeMille, 2000, p. 74). In most cases, we should focus on *healing, whole,* or *broken* stories and forgo spending much time with *bent* ones. The worth of movies can also be evaluated in this way.

As students get older and become more mature in their worldview development, you can begin to introduce them to live individuals who do not share a biblical worldview. This does not have to be an in-your-face clash of worldviews. In fact, it's better if it's not; I've found that the full-frontal assault method doesn't really work to positively shape desires. Instead those kinds of confrontations tend to make people defensive, which has little positive effect. Effective exposure like I'm describing is much more nuanced and subtle, at least while the interaction is happening.

Recently, I was at a meeting in which I regretted not having a student or two along with me because it would have been an ideal example of what I'm talking about. A colleague and I were visiting a local nature conservancy to discuss ways our school could partner with them for practical service-learning experiences. As we talked with the executive director of the conservancy, I noted how several of his underlying assumptions blatantly contradicted a biblical worldview. He espoused assumptions about naturalistic evolution and a sense of worshipping the environment instead of stewarding it for the glory of God. Of course, in that moment it would not have been appropriate for me to confront his secular worldview. However, had some students been in the meeting, we could have debriefed the meeting afterwards to prompt them to think deeply about how this man's basic worldview assumptions guided his day-to-day actions. Sometimes, just a simple conversation with an unbeliever can provide much fodder for worldview development.

> Though fallen and marred by the sinful nature, even "bad" people can't help but think, desire, and do good because the image of God in a person cannot be fully stamped out.

Another way to interact with people from different worldviews is to invite them into your class. You'd be the one to know if your class is prepared for such an interaction, but as a rule of thumb, I'd reserve this kind of interaction for older students. If you're studying some aspect of culture, invite into your class someone who approaches that aspect from a decidedly unchristian perspective. Explain beforehand to your class why you're inviting this person. Prepare your students to exhibit the utmost respect and decorum, instructing them to not contradict the guest. Instead, they can be prepared in advance with good questions to ask.

For instance, you might invite a local elected official into a civics class. Encourage the students to prepare a series of questions about current issues in your community. These questions could address traffic challenges, multifamily housing zoning issues, and caring for the poor. Through answers to these questions, it's certain the guest's worldview would leak through. Students should be alert and carefully listening for heart inclinations, assumptions, and behavioral prescriptions that contradict a biblical worldview. After the interaction, you can discuss with your students what they think the person's core desires are. Talk about the beliefs that became apparent and how suggestions for action demonstrate his or her worldview.

Also, students should be asked to identify where the guest is aligned with a biblical worldview. I've found that such discoveries can seriously challenge our own assumptions about what non-Christians believe, think, and do. This in itself is a valuable worldview lesson. Though fallen and marred by the sinful nature, even "bad" people can't help but think, desire, and do good because the image of God in a person cannot be fully stamped out.

Still another level of engagement would be to invite someone to speak on a hot-button topic such as gay marriage, abortion, euthanasia, or legalized marijuana. This could be for just one class or, like in my example with Dr. Damadian earlier, it could be a special event for multiple classes or grade levels. If you chose to focus on gay marriage, you could begin with a presentation by a local pastor, professor, or church leader who could effectively unpack the biblical perspective on marriage. After that presentation, you would want to debrief with your students to ensure they have a good grasp of the biblical view. Then, after some time elapses, you could invite someone to speak from a pro-gay-marriage perspective. Of course, that person would need to understand what you're doing and agree to speak on those terms. Also, you would be wise to inform parents of what you're doing. (I'm also assuming you know you'd need support from your administration to do something like this.) Students would need to know the ground rules for engagement with your guest, letting them know that this venue is not an opportunity to change the person's mind or vigorously debate the issue. The purpose is to hear directly from someone who has a different view on marriage and to debrief the experience after he or she is finished.

One of the most profound experiences of this nature I have had with students was in Washington, DC, when the Supreme Court was hearing the famous "Jack the Baker" case. You'll likely remember that Colorado baker Jack Phillips refused to bake a custom wedding cake for a gay couple. He found himself in a lengthy legal battle to retain the freedom to express his craft according to his Christian convictions. This case nearly ran him out of business and ultimately took him all the way to the Supreme Court.

> They were able to see the unvarnished, empty philosophies and arguments that had set themselves against the traditional biblical view of marriage. They could also see that the people who hold those views are actual human beings.

I took a group of students to participate in a rally on the steps of the Supreme Court on the day of his hearing. The worldview lessons from that day couldn't have been more profound. When we arrived, we quickly found the "pro-Jack" group and set ourselves to listen to the many short speeches that were being presented, holding our "We've Got Your

Back, Jack" placards. I was thrilled with the cogent, loving, and clear talks that several amazing biblical worldview thinkers presented. John Stonestreet, Russell Moore, Nicole Theis, and others held our attention as they unpacked the implications of Jack's case for the long-term health of religious freedom. This helped to form in each of us a fresh desire to advocate for what is good and right and true in our own lives and our culture. We even got to hear from Jack himself and his brilliant attorney from the Alliance Defending Freedom, Kristen Wagoner.

However, this was not the only learning experience for the day, as others were there as well. Assembled behind our group was a small ensemble from the infamous Westboro Baptist Church, complete with derogatory signs loudly proclaiming the eternal damnation of those who embrace a gay lifestyle. Our students watched in shock as they shouted their slurs. It was one thing to see such protests in quick YouTube clips. It was quite another to see it up close and personal—literally just a few feet away.

Another group, not quite as large as ours, had gathered across the steps from us, complete with their own banners and sound system. They were the pro-gay-marriage crowd, and they were rallying against Jack Phillips. Like our side of the court steps, they had a series of speakers addressing the crowd. However, their speeches were angry, shrill, and full of unfounded conclusions about Christians and our commitment to biblical marriage. Groups of our students would go to "that side" and listen for a while and then return to tell us what they heard. They were able to see the unvarnished, empty philosophies and arguments that had set themselves against the traditional biblical view of marriage. They could also see that the people who hold those views are actual human beings.

Many of our students remarked how that experience of seeing and hearing the pro-gay protesters in comparison with the speakers in our group helped to solidify their own convictions about the biblical view of marriage. It galvanized their desire to defend God's plan for marriage. It was a deeply transformational experience that no amount of time reading worldview materials or sitting through class lectures alone could have prompted.

DEVOTING TIME TO SHAPING DESIRES

Desires are the foundation of a person's worldview, so it makes sense that creating opportunities for student's desires to be shaped is a great place to invest your worldview development efforts. Regular routines (classroom liturgies), role modeling, and exposure to individuals with alternate worldviews have all been shown to contribute to biblical worldview-shaped desires and aims. I highly recommend giving as much time to learning activities designed for shaping desires as to those that are intended to shape thoughts.

In the next chapter, we'll look at how your *pedagogium* can support the kind of processing that has been shown to deepen worldview development. After experiences like we've discussed in this chapter, it's essential that you provide ample opportunity for authentic reflection.

CHAPTER 9

CULTIVATING EXPERIENCES WITHIN YOUR *PEDAGOGIUM*

You may have heard it said that experience is the best teacher. This is one of those time-tested maxims mothers and fathers quote to their children when things get tough. Can you picture it? A teenage son complains about the hard work involved in raking the *entire* yard by hand. Dad philosophically asserts (likely with an accompanying stroke of his chin), "You know, son, experience is the best teacher. Get out there and get to work. Think of how much you'll learn about life, hard work, and character by raking the lawn."

But what if experience can actually be a lousy teacher?

THE ESSENTIAL ELEMENT—PROCESSING

According to professors Sarah Ash and Patti Clayton (2009), if we provide experiences for our students without requiring them to deeply process those experiences, we may be setting them up to

- reinforce things in their minds that are not true;
- develop simplistic solutions to complex problems; and
- generalize inappropriately, based on limited or faulty data.

These results are the exact opposite of what we're trying to help our students do, especially when it comes to developing their worldview. In contrast, we want them

- to become convinced of what is true;
- to recognize the complexity inherent in the real problems human beings face; and
- to draw conclusions and settle questions based on extensive and truthful data, thoughtfully considered.

If we set up experiences as discussed in the last chapter without providing opportunities to process them, we may end up working against the most important goals we have for our students.

Jesus's ministry of teaching was marked by a commitment to processing experiences. He led his disciples to encounter jaw-dropping, paradigm-busting experiences like feeding thousands from virtually nothing, healing a man born blind, and upending tables loaded with goods and money in the temple courts. But he also regularly pulled away from the action to process those experiences with his pupils. They discussed, dissected, and even debated the meaning of what they had seen, heard, and done. This created a powerful iterative cycle of experience followed by processing. The truth proclaimed from within his curriculum of action was matched with a curriculum of processing where learning took root and, over time, transformed a band of misfit learners into world changers. A steady rhythm of experience and processing was featured prominently in the *pedagogium* Jesus created for his disciples.

Here's a simple example of how experience without effective processing can be detrimental to learning. Think about a new driver—we'll call her Sharon—who had her first car accident. At a stoplight, Sharon wasn't paying enough attention to the line of traffic in front of her. She carelessly rolled forward and nudged a truck in front of her. It wasn't a major accident, but she did crumple the hood of her car and puncture her radiator. Unfortunately, her car wasn't worth what it would have cost to repair. So Sharon found herself without a ride.

Thankfully, Sharon's parents understood and saw this unhappy incident as a learning opportunity, helping her process her accident. They asked insightful questions:

- What exactly happened?
- What were you thinking or doing while waiting for the light to change?
- What did you learn from this accident?
- How could you have prevented this from happening?
- What will you do next time you're stopped in a line of traffic at a stoplight?
- What do you need to be on guard against to avoid this kind of thing happening again?

> When processing is well designed, it promotes deeper learning, "including problem-solving skills, higher order reasoning, integrative thinking, goal clarification, openness to new ideas, ability to adopt new perspectives, and systematic thinking."

Sharon's parents walked her through three important steps to process her experience, and we'll look at these steps later in this chapter. For now, though, let's think more about Sharon's story. Since her parents helped her process her experience, it's likely she learned several things from her mishap. Perhaps she learned to be more aware of her surroundings while driving, even when stationary. Maybe she learned how distracting a cell phone or stereo can be. She certainly learned that an accident involves more than damage to a car—it involves money, and usually lots of it.

But what if Sharon's mom and dad had not prompted Sharon to reflect on her mishap? Their anger, frustration, fear, or I-told-you-so attitude could have short-circuited the enormously helpful process of reflecting on her experience. If she hadn't processed the accident with Mom and Dad, she may have blamed someone else for her poor misfortune ("If that truck hadn't been in front of me . . ."). Or maybe she would have just ignored the accident and went on with a sigh and an "Oh well, these things happen" and then quickly focused on getting a different car. Without deeply thinking about what happened, why it happened, and what she could learn from it, Sharon would have suffered from what T. S. Eliot (1943) warned against in the second stanza of his poem, *The Dry Salvages*: having the experience but missing the meaning.

In the realm of education, the research on the value of processing experiences is extensive. It all points to the importance of taking time to think through, discuss and debate, write about, use, and generally reflect on what one is learning. Professors Ash and Clayton summarize this well when they say, "Learning . . . does not happen maximally through experience alone, but rather as a result of thinking about—reflecting on—it." They go on to quote another researcher who sharpens the point even more by saying, "When reflection on experience is weak, students' 'learning' may be 'haphazard, accidental, and superficial.'" To the contrary, when processing is well designed, it promotes deeper learning, "including problem-solving skills, higher order reasoning, integrative thinking, goal clarification, openness to new ideas, ability to adopt new perspectives, and systematic thinking" (Ash and Clayton, 2009, p. 27). Processing seems to be the "secret sauce" to deeper learning.

I discovered this same principle when working with the young adults in my research. Across the board, each one cited processing their experiences as the key to their growth in a biblical worldview. Of course, they didn't use the formal "edu-speak," like the scholars I mentioned above. But they did list a whole range of go-to habits they employed to figure out what their experiences meant and how they could learn from them.

Taking a cue from the habits of my young adult friends, we can identify several key means of processing experiences. These include conversations with peers, reflection, and serving others. Remember, in this book we've considered how a biblical worldview was shaped in the young adults in my study. Now we're applying what we learned from them to the kinds of learning experiences we should be creating for our students. Ideally, these learning experiences will contribute to our students' current worldview development and encourage the formation of consistent habits that will serve them for a lifetime.

CONVERSATIONS WITH PEERS

Not surprisingly, talking with peers was by far the most common way the young adults in my study processed their experiences. This could happen casually over coffee at Starbucks or in a specific and intentional conversation for the purpose of discussing a challenge. They would most often talk with friends to figure out what their experiences meant and how they could learn from them. Worldview development flourishes in a climate of good conversations. When students graduate from our schools, they will be well ahead if they are well practiced in having meaningful conversations with friends.

Unfortunately, productive conversation is a lost art. Perhaps it's becoming even more lost as a result of the ubiquitous technology that has replaced face-to-face connections. How many times have you asked your own children if they talked to a certain person about something, and they said they did? Only later you find out they had merely texted the equivalent of a few monosyllabic grunts back and forth. To buck this trend, a teacher concerned with biblical worldview development will seek to facilitate practice in conversation, even in the youngest learners.

Preschoolers, who are still experimenting with language and vocabulary, can be encouraged to use words to express themselves. This works especially in those tense moments when possession of a plaything is in dispute. They can be required to greet each other by name at the start of the day and refer to one another by name throughout the day. Show and tell can occasionally involve teacher-brokered conversations between students. As appropriate, the teacher can prompt students to ask questions of one another.

Many of these same skills can be practiced in the younger elementary years as students grow in their relational and conversational competencies. Requiring students to use one another's names and facilitating conversations are only the beginning. As soon as practical, teachers should get young students talking to one another specifically about what they're learning. But keep in mind, students need significant guidance in the art of conversation. Many times you will need to give them words to say and questions to ask, as these skills do not come naturally for most children.

One of the handiest techniques for sparking conversation among students is what has become known as the "pair/share method." The teacher gives the students a prompt of some sort that will get them to think about what they are learning. For the youngest grades, this might sound like, "Think about what we just learned in math. When you add two more marbles to the two marbles you already you have, you now have four marbles. Take a few moments to think about this in your head and identify a real-life situation in which you added something to something else and got more of what you had." After a *short* span of time (measured in seconds for young students) the teacher might say, "Now turn to your table buddy and tell him or her about that other real-life addition problem."

As I mentioned before, you'll likely have to support these kinds of micro-conversations quite a bit, listening to students and redirecting or encouraging them to stay focused. Your goal is not so much to achieve fluid, meaningful conversations right away. Rather, you want to create an environment that is conducive to talking about learning. This gives your students practice in talking about what they learn. Ultimately, this kind of environment can shape in your students a tendency to talk about learning and an expectation that discussion is a vital part of learning.

> If you find yourself doing the lion's share of talking during most of your classes, you're probably missing many opportunities to get your students talking to one another.

As students get older, the discussion prompts can become more sophisticated. For instance, after recess, invite your older elementary students to spend one minute telling their friends about their favorite and least-favorite element of the games they played. All field trips should include prompts for peer discussions about what they saw and heard. After a third-grade trip to the local botanical gardens, students can be expected to share about three new plants they hadn't seen before.

To aid in post-experience conversations, students can be told beforehand they will be required to discuss their experiences with their peers. This also helps students to be aware that they will be having experiences worthy of their attention. I find many elementary students rush through activities, especially on field trips. They have no meaningful awareness they're experiencing something new, which of course makes post-experience processing virtually impossible.

Through the middle school and high school years, learning-centered discussions with peers should become more significant and more common. Many teachers use exit tickets for the close of class. An exit ticket is a concluding activity that, once completed, "allows" students to leave class. This could include a prompt to talk with a friend about the hardest topic or idea encountered in class that particular day. Students enhance awareness of their challenges by putting them into words.

By high school, students should come to expect they will be talking in class. As a teacher, you should be constantly working to remove yourself from the central mediating role in discussions. If you find yourself doing the lion's share of talking during most of your classes, you're probably missing many opportunities to get your students talking to one another. Remember, this isn't merely to fill your class with activity and sound. It's to provide lots of practice in the most common way they will be processing their life experiences as they develop their worldview.

REFLECTION

Another means by which a person can process experiences is through the discipline of reflection. According to the Oxford English Dictionary, *to reflect* means to ponder or go back over a thought or idea. The etymology of the word *reflect* hearkens back to when the word was most often used to describe the process of literally bending, turning, or folding an object back on itself. I like the imagery here—it's like folding bread dough over and over on itself in the process of kneading. When a person deeply considers an experience or idea, it's a process similar to kneading dough and involves mental bending, pressing, turning, and folding. This is the preparation for solidifying new learning, insights, or a change in direction.

The kind of mental exertion necessary for effective reflection is hard. It can be easy to skip over this crucial discipline in favor of easier activities. John Piper (2013, p. 96) captures the challenge of deep reflection: "Insight or understanding is the product of intensive, headache-producing meditation." And if it wasn't bad enough that reflection itself is hard, we live in a culture that tends not to prize deep thought all that much. Instead, society opts for unverified sound bites and social media rants. However, I found in my research that, for young adults with a strongly developing worldview, deep thinking about their experiences was an irreplaceable discipline.

> Reflection is, according to Dewey (1910, p. 6), "active, persistent and careful consideration of any belief or supposed form of knowledge in the light of the grounds that support it and the further conclusions to which it tends."

According to Ash and Clayton (2009), reflection is a key part of learning and can take many different shapes and forms. What's consistent across all forms of effective reflection is a sustained mental activity that helps students make meaning of what they're learning. This meaning-making process helps to permanently "install" the products of learning in the minds and hearts of a person. Merely learning facts, procedures, or concepts without understanding their meaning—especially as students get older—tends to produce shallow learning.

You'll note that I added an important qualifier in that last sentence. The importance of grasping meaning increases as students get older. In the younger years, much learning happens without students truly understanding what they're learning, and that's okay. This applies to worldview development as well. Much of early worldview development is not marked by deep understanding. Rather, the early years can be pictured as the season when students are provided with the basic tools they'll need for more advanced worldview development later. This happens even before they understand the whys behind what they're learning and doing.

Unfortunately, reflection doesn't come naturally for most students. You may have a few unique students who are naturally reflective. When you teach something, they automatically think about what you presented to make sure they understood. These students are rare, so most students need support to develop the habit of reflecting on their learning.

Reflection is more than weekly journal assignments in English, one of the more common ways teachers build reflection into their classes. Such assignments are an important aid in learning to write well, since students only become better writers as they write. However, journal writing may or may not actually be the kind of robust reflection that fuels worldview development. When I talk about reflection as meaning making, it's much more than a weekly prompt to get students writing regularly: "Write about the best thing that happened this week," or "What are you looking forward to this year in school?" These prompts may indeed help to develop the habit of thinking about experience, but I find English teachers primarily intend to get students to put pen to paper (or fingers to the keyboard), which is certainly a worthy and necessary objective.

So if reflection is more than journal writing in English class, what is it? Reflection is, according to Dewey (1910, p. 6), "active, persistent and careful consideration of any belief or supposed form of knowledge in the light of the grounds that support it and the further conclusions to which it tends." While Dewey actively campaigned against many of the tenets of a biblical worldview, he nailed it when it comes to a definition of reflection. (I love when someone who doesn't share a biblical worldview is spot-on with an idea or truth.) Schön (1983, p. 281) adds that reflection is "a continual interweaving of thinking and doing." If we combine these two definitions, we can conclude that reflection must be

- a regular feature of learning,
- carefully planned and executed to require age-appropriate depth of thought about what is being learned,
- woven seamlessly together with experience (whether the experience of a field trip or a math lesson),
- evaluative in nature,
- grounded in (or connected to) what one has already learned to be true, and
- ideally leading to personal commitments about how to approach other experiences or learning opportunities in the future.

If you string those phrases together into a comprehensive definition of reflection, it can sound pretty long and intimidating.[11] Another less-technical way to define reflection could be to think about experiences in order to understand what they mean and to generate ideas for how learning should impact the approach and response to future experiences. This is precisely how my friends in the worldview development study utilized reflective practices as they struggled through new experiences. There is great value in contextualizing that same process for students at every stage of their development. Not only will doing so promote deeper learning, it can also develop a reflective approach to all their experiences, which will serve them well throughout their lives.

Reflection can take many forms, such as journaling, discussions, creating artwork or music, writing stories or poetry, drama, mini-construction projects such as dioramas, and so on. There's not one go-to method for helping students think about what they're learning. Actually, the method you choose is not as critical as the prompts you use to guide your students' reflection. Just about any task can be harnessed as a reflection activity.

Professors Ash and Clayton (2009) distilled much of the research on reflection down to a handy four-letter acronym: DEAL. It summarizes what makes reflection most effective. I've adapted and added to it to help direct our efforts at facilitating reflection:

D: *Description* of a student's experiences in an objective and detailed manner

E: *Examination/evaluation* of those experiences in light of learning objectives and in light of what students already know to be true

AL: *Articulation of Learning*, including commitments for future action

The DEAL acronym is a helpful guide in creating reflection activities for your students. The experiences mentioned in *description* can be anything from a class lesson to a field trip. The first step in effective reflection is to have students describe their experience in as much detail as possible and practical. The second step (*examination/*

> Good questions will be open-ended, leaving as much room as possible for students to explore many aspects of their learning.

evaluation) invites students to evaluate their experiences according to two measures: stated learning objectives and connection to what they already know to be true. Finally, in the *articulation of learning* step, students are challenged to describe exactly what they learned and to forecast how this new learning will be applied in future experiences.

A critical factor in crafting effective reflection exercises is utilizing good questions that will prompt students appropriately. It is not sufficient to say, "Okay, class, that was a hard Spanish lesson. Take a few minutes to write down what you learned." The prompts you use for reflection exercises should be well thought out so they fit the DEAL framework and are also developmentally appropriate.

The following list contains several sample prompts that could be used as templates for the prompts you create in each of the three steps of the DEAL paradigm:

D:

- Describe your experience with _____.
- What did you learn in this lesson and how did you learn it?
- Describe what you did and how you felt in this scenario.

E:

- Explain how what you learned in this lesson connects to what you already know.
- How did this assignment/experience help you to understand _____ in a deeper way?

- Why does it matter that you learned/experienced this?
- How does what you learned/experienced connect to God's view of the world?

AL:

- What will you do the next time you encounter a lesson/experience like this?
- What do you still need to learn about _____?
- How can you prepare yourself for the next time you encounter a lesson/experience like this?
- How does it benefit you to have experienced/learned this?
- Where else can you apply what you learned in this lesson/experience?

The options for good reflection-prompting questions are practically limitless. As you practice implementing reflection exercises in your class, you'll find questions and types of questions that work well and those that don't yield great results. In general, good questions will be open-ended, leaving as much room as possible for students to explore many aspects of their learning. Learning to ask good open-ended questions is actually a great conversational skill to learn as a teacher. For instance, instead of asking "Did you enjoy that book?" you could say, "What did you like about that book?" Or, in place of "Was it easy to pay attention in chapel today?" try "What was it like to stay focused during chapel today?" Simple shifts in asking questions can elicit more robust and thoughtful reflection from your students.

Reflection exercises can be used both for academic learning objectives as well as character and behavioral objectives and should be planned in advance. While you can certainly jump in with reflection exercises in the spur of the moment to fill time or when an ideal reflection moment pops up, the most effective reflection exercises will be planned ahead and assessed.

Here are a few examples of reflection exercises that can be used at various grade levels. As you read through the case stories, try to identify the aspects of the DEAL reflection framework that you see in operation.

1. Preschool

After spending time at the playground, a preschool teacher gathered her students in a circle. She asked them to name their favorite activity on the playground that day. After getting a few responses, the teacher asked two of the more verbal students a few questions to get them to describe their favorite activity in a bit more detail. She affirmed the students for each new detail they provided. Then the teacher asked the students to think about what they would like to do during playground time later that day. She had a few students share their ideas.

> He didn't merely want them to say what was hard. He wanted them to describe it, including how they felt while doing it and why it was hard.

2. Early Elementary

After a first-grade history lesson on Early American westward expansion, the teacher asked students to draw a picture of a pioneer family. The teacher instructed them to include things they'd need to take with them if they were traveling to a new home. After completing the pictures, students spent time imagining how they would feel if their mom and dad told them they would be moving to a new place. The teacher asked a few children to share how they would feel and to also show and describe their picture to the rest of the class. A few students expressed negative feelings about moving. The teacher affirmed that God is with them and that we can trust God in times when we're afraid. Finally, the teacher asked her students how they can learn to rely on God in times when they are afraid. She affirmed and clarified the positive strategies the students mentioned.

3. Late Elementary

Students in a fourth-grade class went on a field/service trip to a local nature preserve to help maintain the preserve's woodland walkways. The teacher asked the students to think about the most difficult part of the project and to be prepared to write down their thoughts when they returned. Once back in class, the teacher gave each student a piece of paper with a prompt: "The hardest part of working at the preserve today was . . ." Before the students began writing, the teacher explained he didn't merely want them to say what was hard. He wanted them to describe it, including how they felt while doing it and why it was hard.

After the students finished answering the prompt, the teacher called everyone into a circle to review their answers. He asked students questions as they shared to deepen their assessment of why certain things were hard to do. Next, he asked them to think about how they would approach working at the preserve next time, knowing what they knew about what it will involve. Finally, he instructed each student to turn to a buddy to share their thoughts about how the work at the preserve will go next time.

4. Middle School

For a seventh grade Spanish class, the teacher set aside one entire class period every two weeks as "reflection day." He knew middle school students can tend to simply deliver what is asked of them in Spanish without really thinking deeply about what they're learning. To start one of their reflection days, the teacher gave students a few minutes to jot down as many topics and concepts from the previous two weeks as they could remember. Toward the close of the time allotment for the brainstorming, the teacher told them they should have at least five or six items listed.

After confirming that students had the required number of items on their lists, the teacher instructed them to rank their items in order of easiest to hardest to learn. Once that was completed, students turned to a friend to compare lists and rankings. Next, each pair of students combined their lists into one new list. Then together they ranked them in order of importance, with one being the most important concept they learned and so on.

> Your goal in requiring reflection is twofold: to deepen current learning and to develop in students processing skills that can lead to a reflective lifestyle, which is a key element in worldview development.

The teacher then told them to take the most important item on their combined list and find their class notes or textbook section on that subject to review what they need to learn about that concept. After reviewing the material, the teacher required the students to write down three reminders about the concept they would need to keep in mind in order to remember what they had learned. Finally, the teacher had each pair of students join with another pair to share their most important concepts and their reminders. To close the reflection day, the teacher asked one or two groups to share their work with the rest of the class. Then he led a brief discussion to brainstorm how the reminders could be applied in other classes besides Spanish.

5. High School

An eleventh-grade AP biology class finished a unit on the mathematical models that support evolution. For homework, the teacher assigned a reflection assignment that involved a two-page essay in response to the unit. Instructions for the essay included the following prompts:

1. Summarize the major mathematical models that our textbook suggests support evolution in enough detail so that someone who is not familiar with them could understand what you're saying.

2. Think about what our class text assumed about the origin of life, and briefly compare one or two of those assumptions to what you know about the biblical account of the origin of life.

3. Imagine you are in a biology class in a secular college. How would you respond to a professor who opened class by saying this? "If you are one of those right-wing fundamentalist Christians, please be sure to leave your religion at home. This is a science class, not a philosophy class." Write a brief, respectful response to your professor as if you were writing him a personal note.

While these examples are fictional, they demonstrate what effective reflection exercises can look like. Keep in mind, your goal in requiring reflection is twofold: to deepen current learning and to develop in students processing skills that can lead to a reflective lifestyle, which is a key element in worldview development.

SERVING OTHERS

One of the best ways to get me to learn a skill or concept and learn it quickly is to tell me I have to teach it. There's something powerful in the pressure to have something of worth to pass on to someone else. My young adult friends from my research confirmed this reality. They suggested that serving others in ministry or as mentors accelerated their own worldview development. Whether it was as campus ministry leaders or mentors to younger students, they saw a direct connection between helping others develop their worldview and the growth of their own.

One form of serving others that was particularly helpful to my friends was being called upon to articulate their beliefs to others. Applying this to K–12 students, you can create opportunities for students of all ages to be consistently sharing what they're learning not only with peers, but also with younger students. A second-grade teacher can have her students regularly read out loud to kindergarten students. For added worldview development value, the books could be children's books specifically written about worldview issues, such as Champ Thornton's *Why Do We Say Goodnight?* A seventh-grade life science class can be called upon to help third graders with a lab. A tenth-grade Spanish III class can visit a Spanish I class to share tips for how to be successful in learning Spanish. Twelfth-grade students could be challenged to submit an application to speak in chapel.

> Processing experiences is vital to good learning, and this extends far beyond academic content and skills alone.

Beyond these planned ways of serving younger students, all students in a school community can be encouraged and expected to look for ways to serve those who are younger than them. A lifestyle of service is obviously consistent with a biblical worldview. The more practice we can give our students in caring for and supporting others, including in their academic learning, the more likely they will become committed to serving others as a part of their own development.

Processing experiences is vital to good learning, and this extends far beyond academic content and skills alone. Young adults who have a maturing biblical worldview consistently derive meaning from their experiences through processing. They do not merely navigate life on autopilot. Providing abundant opportunities for our students to process their experiences, both in and out of the classroom, is another vital way to fashion a *pedagogium* that can prepare them for a lifetime of worldview development. In the next chapter, we'll explore how to create the most engaging learning experiences possible—ones in which students are cognitively, emotionally, and even physically connected to what they're learning.

CHAPTER 10

EMBRACING THE CHAOS OF ENGAGED LEARNING

When you imagine students in an ideal classroom, what do you picture? My picture of the ideal classroom has changed over my years in Christian school leadership. I've come to believe that the deepest, longest-lasting learning occurs in a highly active, highly engaged classroom, though that kind of classroom can sometimes be a bit chaotic. But that wasn't always how I pictured the ideal.

MAXIMUM ENGAGEMENT OVER MAXIMUM ORDER

Back on the first professional development day I had planned as a newly minted head of school, my academic dean and I invited an expert in differentiated learning to provide a day of workshops for our team. He was one of those stand-and-deliver kind of teachers

161

they make movies about. He had worked in the hardest school in his district and saw great success with many of the most challenging students you can imagine. I couldn't wait to meet him in person and have him inspire and equip our teachers.

Before the actual day, Ken visited our campus to go over details for the training and to get a lay of the land. It fell to me to take him on a tour of the building. As we made our way through the science wing, I remember feeling a sense of pride. We passed by classrooms full of model students sitting quietly in their seats, eyes focused on the teacher, and carefully taking notes from the PowerPoint presentation. *It couldn't have gotten any better*, I thought, assuming Ken would be impressed by the decorum and order that marked our classrooms. (I never did ask if he was impressed. But after a day of experiencing his highly engaging and energetic workshops, I'm pretty sure he wasn't.)

> While order and traditional student decorum can be important, they don't equate to deep learning.

Today, I have a different perspective. I now look with a degree of suspicion on classes that are too quiet and orderly. Just the other day, I walked past a classroom with lots of noise wafting into the hallway. Almost automatically, the noise drew me in to investigate the great learning that appeared to be happening. What was supposed to be a quick pop-in ended up being twenty minutes. I marveled at how the teacher engaged the students in an activity requiring their mental, emotional, and physical involvement. If I could snap a picture of my ideal classroom now, that would have been it. A bunch of new ninth graders crowded around several hands-on projects, discussing how to best make a foil boat hold maximum weight in water. They were exploring the kind of thinking skills they would need as they progressed through their Intro to Computer Science class.

So what changed for me? Why the drastic alteration of my educational values? How did maximum engagement come to supplant maximum order as my classroom ideal?

It's really quite simple. Over time, I've come to see that, while order and traditional student decorum can be important, they don't equate to deep learning. Research shows that pristine order and structured lectures requiring students to sit quietly and listen can actually work *against* deep learning (Colby, Ehrlich, Beaumont, & Stephens, 2003). Doing so makes it easy to completely disengage while appearing to pay attention. That makes intuitive sense and the most basic (and perhaps most often cited) research supports this

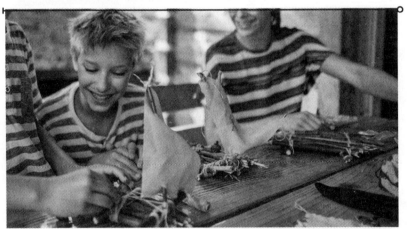

fact. After twenty-four hours, students retain about 5 percent of what they heard in a lecture, 10 percent of what they read, 50 percent of what they learned through discussion, and 90 percent of what they used right away or taught to others (Sousa, 2006). Sousa goes on to observe that "despite the impressive amount of evidence about how little students retain from lecture, it continues to be the most prevalent method of teaching, especially in secondary and higher education" (p. 94). Now, as a teacher, I start getting antsy if my students merely sit quietly absorbing the information I'm dispensing. I wonder whether there's any learning actually happening.

A favorite proverb of mine says, "Where there are no oxen, the manger [stall] is clean, but abundant crops come by the strength of an ox" (Proverbs 14:4). This short axiom from Solomon has many applications. However, in the learning context, it reminds us that "neat and clean" means delivering lectures with our students passively taking it in while not engaging with it. But the "mess" of student engagement often accomplishes much more.

Jesus knew this age-old pedagogical principle well. He understood that maximum learning comes from maximum involvement of all a person's dimensions: heart, mind, and body. When he wanted to teach his disciples about trusting God for provision of all that they need, he didn't only sit them down for a good lecture. Yes, he did tell them (in the Sermon on the Mount) that they need not worry about what they would eat or what they would wear. But that lecture-based teaching preceded numerous situations in which they could taste, feel, and even joyfully participate in his supernatural provision.

The feeding of the five thousand and the four thousand was about the urgent need to care for the multitudes who were following him. But it was also classic engaged learning. He confronted the disciples with a challenge beyond their ability to solve. Then they were intimately involved in seeing God's provision come to hungry throngs. Their future ability to trust God in all things as they turned the world upside down at great personal risk was largely dependent on what they learned. They were authentically engaged in Jesus's *pedagogium*, complete with bits of fish under their fingernails and basketsful of extra bread.

ACTIVE INVOLVEMENT IN THE DEVELOPMENT PROCESS

Going back to the young adults in my research, one of the central characteristics of those with a maturing biblical worldview is active involvement in the development process. They were not simply passive receptors of knowledge and they certainly didn't sit on the sidelines, while experiences shuffled by without inviting engagement. They were actors in the process of their own worldview development, and they personally owned that process. Worldview development was something they *did*, not something that *happened to them.*

Unfortunately, learning in many classrooms can look more like something that happens to students rather than something they actively do. This tendency to structure our classrooms and our lessons in ways that engender passivity may very well be setting up our students for a difficult awakening. When they strike out into adulthood, they find that learning is not neatly packaged and hand-delivered to them. If we expect our students to take ownership of their worldview development, we need to help them take appropriate ownership of their learning now. This is facilitated in part by creating learning experiences that require active engagement.

There's also a credibility issue here. We often tell our students they need to learn "in order to . . ." This formula is essentially saying that learning is preparation for some kind of doing. Maybe we don't realize what we're saying when we use this formula, and perhaps we're just reaching for something to motivate our students to pay attention and learn. But at its core, learning should result not just in some kind of cognitive achievement. It has to be demonstrated in appropriate doing which should be accompanied by a desire for the doing. And if doing is the aim of learning, then our credibility is at stake if we offer learning experiences that require only passive reception as opposed to active engagement.

The level of student engagement can be hard to determine, but assessing engagement can be made easier when we have a good working definition of engagement in hand. I describe engagement as the degree to which my students are demonstrating active cognitive, emotional, or behavioral connections with the content being learned. To aid in thinking more specifically about what engaged learning looks like, I've developed the following rubric which details various levels of engagement (adapted from Heick).

Engagement Level	Indicators
Authentic Engagement	• Clearly exhibits various dimensions of activity (cognitive, emotional, and physical) • Demonstrates a joyful and proactive ethos • Self-directed and self-motivated • Suggests or pursues options for transferring knowledge or skills to other domains • Encourages others to learn—directly and by example • Gets "caught up" in learning • Generates ideas to take learning "one step further"
Transactional Engagement	• Complies with teacher directions • Motivated by grades or teacher commendation • Does what is needed for compliance • Occasionally contributes to classroom discussions
Limited Engagement	• Demonstrates sporadic, inconsistent engagement • Can go for long periods of time without saying anything • Begrudgingly participates when required • May follow the crowd—if they're engaged, they may engage to be accepted by peers

Disengagement	• Demonstrates no interest in learning activities • Avoids contact with teacher (eye contact or otherwise) • Does not follow simple directions during class • Can be a distraction to other students who are more engaged
Rebellion	• Purposely disrupts others from learning • Mocks teacher attempts to engage him or others • Mocks other students who engage in learning • Exhibits a negative or combative attitude when asked to participate

Creating a *pedagogium* that is marked by engagement with learning can be difficult, especially if you're attempting to transition a group of older students to embrace an expectation of engagement. Unfortunately, many students have been lulled into a pattern of transactional engagement in which they supply completed assignments in exchange for good grades. To make matters worse, transactional engagement can masquerade as authentic engagement, and it takes a discerning teacher or observer to perceive the difference.

Work together with school leadership and your close colleagues, so your classroom is not isolated from a broader school culture that does not prize engagement.

This conundrum strikes at the very heart of one of our culture's most dearly held educational values. This view considers the purpose of education to be earning good grades so students will be equipped to get good grades next year. Ultimately they'll graduate from high school with good grades, so they can go to a good college (and perhaps get a scholarship!). Then they can graduate from college with good grades and then get a well-paying job. And this crazy series of expectations starts even with our youngest learners. I've known plenty of early elementary students (and their parents) who have been deeply stressed by the red letter or number on the top of their homework papers. I'd much prefer for them and their parents to be concerned about whether they love learning!

Consider yourself warned: if you begin to require authentic engagement from your students, you'll be working against years of educational inertia. For many students, they'll perceive this as a threat to the transactional system they've come to thrive in and depend on. This reality makes it all the more important that you do not make these changes on your own. Work together with school leadership and your close colleagues, so your classroom is not isolated from a broader school culture that does not prize engagement.

In my undergraduate New Testament course, I address this issue in the first session. I let my students know the class will not exclusively be about my dispensing information to them. It will be *their* job to pursue information through the reading and the other means of acquiring knowledge that I will arrange (including my lectures). *My* job, I tell them, is to create experiences for them that will require them to deeply engage with our course content. As a result, they can expect to truly change as a result of participating in learning.

While some students get excited about the prospects of not having to sit through hours of lectures, I do find quite a few of them are put off by my shaking up the transactional system they've come to expect. Over time, though, most of them (as long as they're not living in the disengaged or rebellion levels of engagement) come around and later thank me for creating a *pedagogium* like that. (Okay, they don't use that word, but they do express appreciation for the way I run the class.)

I find that many teachers object to focusing on engaged learning. They picture it as some kind of postmodern relinquishment of authority in the classroom or a free-for-all pooling of students' ignorance. But creating an environment rich with student engagement does not diminish my role in the classroom, nor is it an excuse to be sloppy in my study. I'm not stepping away from my responsibility to deeply understand and communicate the knowledge about the subject they're expected to master. Just the opposite is true. Having a classroom marked by authentic engagement requires me to be very much on top of my subject matter. I'll likely be challenged with what students are learning, and it can be tough to stay a few steps ahead of a group of excited, self-motivated learners. It's much easier to fill class time with the sound of my voice and simply expect students to absorb what I'm saying in preparation for being tested on it.

FIVE WAYS TO ENGAGE

I hope you can see how important it is to create an environment of engagement for your students, but not only for the purposes of today. Think forward to the young adult years when your students will be initiated into the often-frightful world of "adulting." They'll have no choice but to engage what comes their way. Will Richardson (2016) of Modern Learners says it this way: "Students moving into adulthood today need more than anything else to be voracious, passionate learners, adept at creating their own personal learning curriculum, finding their own teachers to help mentor and guide them in their efforts, and connecting with other learners with whom they can collaborate and create" (p. 25). While Richardson was not talking about young adults developing a biblical worldview, he's spot-on with what I discovered in my research with Christian young adults. Providing an engaged learning environment in every class at every grade level builds in students a sense of ownership of their learning. Over time, it nurtures a commitment to authentic learning that is active and self-motivated.

The balance of this chapter will provide examples of what engaged learning can look like in and out of the classroom. For the first few of these examples, I'm indebted to Professors Bill and Persida Himmele of Millersville University. They have championed the cause of engaged learning through their research and their highly acclaimed book, *Total Participation Techniques.*[12]

1. Think-Pair-Share

> In this day when health experts call sitting the new smoking, we should take every opportunity to get our students up and out of their chairs to get their blood circulating to their brains.

The Think-Pair-Share method is a simple way to ensure students are sticking with the teacher in class. After a brief lecture, reading, video, or other form of input, the teacher provides a prompt that requires all students to reflect on their learning. Instead of the customary raising of hands that keeps just a few students engaged in learning, the teacher instructs all the students to think for a moment to formulate a response. Then students are instructed to turn to a partner to talk about their responses one on one.

Himmele and Himmele (2017) suggest that sparking learning by asking for volunteers to respond to a prompt with raised hands actually only serves the ones who raise their hands. Generally, everyone else checks out. But even for the bold hand raisers, many prompts are not followed by enough time for students to formulate thoughtful responses. So the answers given can often be fairly shallow. Think-Pair-Share gets everyone thinking about a prompt and preparing their answer before being asked to share it—that's engagement. After going through Think-Pair-Share, you can ask specific pairs to share their insights with the rest of the class to facilitate broader discussion. But if you want everyone involved in learning, make sure you don't start with class-wide discussion. You'll likely have the same few talking with everyone else passively listening at best or completely checking out at worst.

A slight variation on Think-Pair-Share is to have students draw a picture to respond to a prompt instead of preparing a verbal answer. Then when they are sharing with their partner, they show the picture and describe what it means. After the sharing time, students can all go to the whiteboard or a blank wall and post their pictures for all to see. The teacher can review some of the pictures, asking for clarity from individual students as necessary. This is a variation on what the Himmeles call the Chalkboard Splash.

2. Chalkboard Splash

The Chalkboard Splash not only nurtures cognitive engagement but physical engagement as well. One researcher shadowed a group of high school students for a few days and discovered those students spent about 90 percent of their school days sitting in chairs listening to lectures (Himmele and Himmele, 2017). In this day when health experts call sitting the new smoking, we should take every opportunity to get our students up and out of their chairs to get their blood circulating to their brains. Injecting some quick physical movement into a class is a great way to increase cognitive and emotional engagement and break the boredom.

For this technique, students are provided with a sentence starter or prompt related to what they are learning. Students first jot down their ideas on their own, after they've had an opportunity to think through their response. After a set amount of time, the teacher instructs everyone to go to the whiteboard to copy their responses in random spots, with a limit of ten to fifteen words. When I've done this, it always seems to elicit emotional engagement too. Students have fun writing on the board and laughing while they observe what others are writing.

After everyone finishes writing their responses, depending on the age and maturity of the students, they walk around and analyze others' responses. They can jot down similarities and differences among what their peers have written. Especially fun is being challenged to find statements or responses that surprise the students. After walking and analyzing, the teacher can ask students to get into small groups to share their analysis.

Another Chalkboard Splash variety involves asking students to classify facts or ideas. Each student is given a few sticky notes and directed to write down several facts or concepts related to some central concept. Then the teacher creates two or more large boxes on the white board, labeling them with broad categories. The students then place their sticky notes on the board, based on how they think their responses should be categorized. For instance, after jotting down facts and concepts related to the Civil War, students could be asked to categorize their responses by posting their notes in boxes on the whiteboard: "Causes of the War," "Struggling through the Conflict," or "Impact of the War." As with the other examples, the exercise should be wrapped up with the teacher reading and reviewing the students' categorizations.

The beauty of the Chalkboard Splash is twofold. First, it keeps students engaged with novel ways to list, evaluate, and categorize information. Second, it gives students a constructive reason to get out of their seats to get their blood circulating and give them a change of pace. Having an entire class up at the whiteboard may need to be managed creatively to prevent chaos. But the value of the different ways you can use the Chalkboard Splash is certainly worth the extra traffic control you'll need to do. And you can use the Chalkboard Splash with any age student, as you can adjust the prompt to whatever you're studying to be age appropriate.

3. Debate Team Carousel

The Debate Team Carousel is an engaged learning tool that works for older students who are capable of deeper processing and evaluation. I've used it successfully with my undergraduate students and adult learners. It can be used throughout high school and perhaps in an advanced middle school class. It's one of my favorites for getting students to engage with multiple viewpoints on an issue. As we discussed earlier, seeing and analyzing other perspectives not consistent with a biblical worldview is an important gateway for developing one's own worldview.

The Debate Team Carousel (Himmele and Himmele, 2017, p. 108) utilizes a simple template that the teacher prepares for the students in advance. It is intended to be passed from student to student so that each box is completed by a different person. The template is a simple grid with four equal boxes (which takes

> Requiring students to think deeply about their own ideas and respectfully engage opposing ideas is truly the stuff of worldview development.

up the entire page) labeled as follows: The first box says, "Give your opinion and explain your rationale." The second box says, "Read your classmate's response from box one. In this box, add another reason that would *support* your classmate's response." The third box says, "In this box, record a reason that might be used to argue *against* what is written in boxes #1 and #2." Finally, the fourth box says, "Read what is written in the three boxes. Add *your opinion* and *your reason* for it in this box."

To begin this activity, create a prompt that will require students to develop their own opinion on a subject or issue. Complexity of the prompts are determined by the maturity of the class and the depth to which the content has been explored by the students. For this activity to be successful, the students' opinions will need to be supportable, meaning they have to have clear rationale for their conclusions. The prompt should be written on the board or projected on a screen so it is readable during the entire activity.

Every student in the class will need a copy of the template. All the students respond to each prompt at the same time. Instruct them to write their name on the top of the paper, and then begin working on box one. After a set amount of time, direct the students to pass their paper to another student (to the right or the next row, for instance). Once students receive another student's template, they begin working on box two. This process will continue until they complete all four boxes on different papers.

After the template is completely filled out, the papers are passed back to their original owners. They will review their peers' work in boxes two through four and think about the arguments for and against the position they originally stated in box one. Give students the opportunity to share their observations and thoughts about their peers' additions to their work. Students whose opinions have changed or been refined as a result of this activity should be encouraged to share with their classmates the reasons for the change.

This is a great activity because it pushes students to think through and defend their own positions with a clear, well-articulated rationale. Additionally, it challenges them to consider opposing viewpoints, even arguing for a viewpoint they may not agree with. In the service of worldview development, this kind of activity can directly support growth in the cognitive and processing skills students will need throughout their lifetime. Remembering my friends in the research study, requiring students to think deeply about their own ideas and respectfully engage opposing ideas is truly the stuff of worldview development.

4. Thumbs Up/Thumbs Down

Thumbs Up/Thumbs Down is a simple tool that I have developed to aid in engaging students when you are using a less active learning method such as a lecture or a video. To create the tool, divide a sheet of paper into four equal quadrants. In the top left quadrant, insert a small thumbs-up icon. In the top right, insert a small thumbs-down. For the bottom left, insert a question mark. Finally, in the bottom right, insert an exclamation point. Each of these small icons represents a set of responses that students may have to the content being presented.

- Thumbs Up—What I agree with or what I like about what I'm hearing/seeing.
- Thumbs Down—What I disagree with or what I don't like about what I'm hearing/seeing.
- Question Mark—What I'd like to know more about or what questions I have about what has been presented.
- Exclamation—My big "takeaways" from what I'm hearing/seeing or what I think is the most important concept(s) or ideas(s).

To use the Thumbs Up/Thumbs Down tool, simply give it to your students prior to a lecture/video/podcast/etc. and explain what they should include in each quadrant. Students can use their completed tool as a means to either discuss their reactions with a peer or with the entire class.

I've found this simple tool to be a fun and effective way to keep students engaged with content that is being presented in class. Additionally, it helps them to prepare to interact with others about what they've heard and seen. And it works with all ages of students, including adult learners.

5. Service-Learning

The previous learning strategies we explored were limited in scope. They're the kinds of methods that can be implemented in individual class periods as stand-alone devices to get students more engaged. Service-learning is a long-term pedagogy that connects instructional objectives with authentically serving the community.

Service-learning takes what students are learning in the classroom and puts it into practice by serving people's needs with what is being learned. Research suggests that service-learning could be a powerhouse pedagogy.

Here are just a few of the research-based outcomes of service learning that Dr. Lynn Swaner and I documented in our previous book on service-learning, *Bring It to Life: Christian Education and the Transformative Power of Service-Learning* (Swaner and Erdvig, 2018):

- **Academic achievement:** Students' academic performance increases; students learn concepts and skills more deeply when they are given opportunities to apply what they're learning to serve others.

- **Civic engagement:** Students get more involved in their local communities, leading to a tendency to continue looking for opportunities to be involved after graduation.

- **Development of beliefs/values:** Students grow in understanding of and commitment to their beliefs and values when they have to live them out in authentic ways.

- **Leadership development:** Students develop the relational and leadership skills needed to effectively work together with a team.

- **Commitment to service:** Students express (verbally and, later in life, behaviorally) a strong commitment to serving others, including a tendency to pursue people-serving vocations.

These are exactly the kinds of biblically shaped results we're looking to produce in our students, right? This list reads like part of the profiles of people who have a solid biblical worldview. They use their intellect well, develop the ability to lead and work on a team, and actively serve others in their local community. This should not come as much of a surprise, though, as the concept of service-learning is built on a thoroughly biblical foundation (Erdvig and Swaner, 2018).

Service-learning's foundation is Christlikeness; his disciples serve because he served first. Additionally, in seeking to develop leaders, we are reminded that Christian leadership is defined by the "law of inversion" in which the one who wishes to be a leader must become a servant. Beyond these, though, there is also the Christian imperative to serve others by meeting their practical needs. James 2:14–26 unpacks the mandate to care for other's needs when we are presented with the opportunity. Finally, Christ's example as a teacher demonstrates the power of seamlessly integrated learning experiences where content is bonded to experience and reflection.

> Effective service-learning involves hands-on projects that meet authentic needs in the community, are sustained over time, and are relational in nature.

But what does service-learning look like in practice? Here are a few examples:

A fourth-grade class adopted a local food pantry, providing basic mathematical/statistical support for the pantry. Students collected and served food to needy individuals and families. At the same time, they applied their growing math skills in purchasing goods, graphing, estimating, and creating spreadsheets. They used their math skills to serve others in the broader context of curing what was broken (hunger, poverty), though only on a person-by-person scale.

Another example is an eleventh-grade English class that studied the literature genre of war stories. Students read, analyzed, and responded to classic war stories, such as *All Quiet on the Western Front*. But they also spent an entire school year deeply connecting with veterans through various visits and small projects. This culminated in a veteran's night where local veterans were invited to a special event, including patriotic, honoring presentations by students. The main purpose of the evening, though, was for pairs of students to interview individual veterans to document their stories. Over the next weeks, these stories became the students' writing assignments. They eventually compiled them into a digital repository that honors and preserves the accounts of the sacrifices of men and women who have served in the military.

These are just two examples of actual projects. Options for connecting service to classroom learning are limited only by the imagination and initiative of teachers and their students.

To be most effective, service-learning projects should generally follow a regular cycle (Erdvig and Swaner, 2018):

- **Classroom learning:** Service-learning projects emerge from the classroom learning objectives that are already in place. Unlike typical community-service requirements that are disconnected from the classroom, service-learning is inextricably linked to what's already being learned. In fact, if the service-learning project is not connected to classroom learning, it's not technically service-learning and loses much of the potential impact on student learning and worldview development.

- **Service Experiences:** Effective service-learning involves hands-on projects that meet authentic needs in the community, are sustained over time, and are relational in nature. Most of the activity in service-learning projects should occur outside the classroom and should involve significant, repeated interaction with people. The service locations and projects are also overtly connected to *creating, cultivating, curbing,* or *curing* to ground the projects in an applied biblical worldview, in addition to classroom content.

- **Reflection:** Harkening back to our earlier discussion about the experience/reflection cycle, reflection in service-learning is key to integrating the learning with personal growth and awareness (Kaye, 2004, p. 11).

Service-learning holds promise not only for enhancing current academic learning through maximal engagement, it is also excellent for current worldview development and as a prompt for future development.[13]

We've covered quite a bit of ground in the last three chapters, describing elements of the *pedagogium* that can effectively support the worldview-development process. But we still have one more teacher-related topic to discuss. And it may very well be the topic you hoped to see when you first picked up this book. In the next chapter, we'll tackle the principles for how to provide extensive, incremental, and subject-based experience with the truth claims and practical application of a biblical worldview.

CHAPTER II

TEACHING FROM A
BIBLICAL
WORLDVIEW

Cue the drum roll—this is likely the chapter you've been waiting for. I've made the point that merging biblical worldview truths with course content is not the whole story. But it certainly is a foundational and essential element of the *pedagogium* we want to create for our students. You can give them plenty of practice in the disciplines they'll need to develop their worldview. You can provide many new experiences coupled with effective reflection. And you can make your classroom learning activities engaging. But without intentionally teaching your subject matter from a biblical worldview perspective, you'll come up short in providing the kinds of classroom experiences that will holistically support your students' worldview development.

UNDERSTANDING MACRO- AND MICRO-PROPOSITIONS

A biblical worldview includes both macro- and micro-propositions of truth. The macro-propositions include answers to the biggest questions about life. The micro-propositions relate to specific topics and arenas of God's grand creation. The macro-propositions answer questions such as follows:

- Who is God?
- What is the nature of the universe?
- Who is man?
- What is man's position in relationship to God and the universe?
- Is there a fixed moral standard for human behavior?
- What is the ultimate purpose of mankind?
- What happens after we die?

These are some of the big universal questions that have occupied sages throughout the millennia, since the dawn of creation. Certainly, these are important concepts to grapple with, and there's likely space in every course to include some discussion around them.

> These truth claims are perfectly suited for every classroom, including all electives and core courses.

However, it's not likely that a fifth-grade math course will need to include instruction on the eternal destiny of man. The macro-propositions of a biblical worldview are more effectively explored in a class designed for that purpose, such as a Bible class that focuses on worldview. I'm pretty sure parents would have a legitimate beef with you if you consumed significant chunks of chemistry class debating the fixed, universal moral standard for human behavior. I'll tackle this idea more in the next chapter, which is addressed to school leaders. It offers suggestions about how to ensure that students are, over time, being exposed to the macro-propositions of a biblical worldview in your school's curriculum.

Micro-propositions, or secondary propositions, are those truth claims that emerge from the macro-propositions and which relate to more specific aspects of the human experience. These truth claims are perfectly suited for every classroom, including all electives and core courses. Let's jump right to an example of a subject-specific truth claim that will help to illustrate what I mean.

Math is often looked at as one of the toughest subjects in which to effectively integrate biblical worldview. So let's take an example micro-proposition from this area, which comes from Christian Overman and Don Johnson (2003, p. 27): "Math enables us to glorify God by doing the 'good works which God prepared beforehand' (Ephesians 2:10) more effectively. (Consider the fields of medicine, agriculture, economics, etc.)" This micro-proposition frames one of the purposes of learning math: to become more skilled in certain areas so a person can do good works that depend on math in some way. Good medicine, good agriculture, and good economics all require proficiency in math. Anytime students master a mathematical concept, they are adding yet another tool in their toolkit for doing good.

This truth claim that math helps us develop skills to glorify God is *secondary*; it emerges from several macro-propositions. These include the following:

- God is the ultimate Creator and Lord of the universe, as he has revealed himself to be in Scripture.

- Mankind's ultimate purpose is to bear God's image and to glorify him.
- Human beings find ultimate fulfillment living in submission to God's good and loving rule.

The challenge for the math teacher is to build bridges in students' understanding so they can learn to perceive the deep connection between math (arithmetic, algebra, and calculus) and God's authority and his design for mankind. This is worthy of time and attention in the math classroom. So how can the math teacher do this?

STARTING WITH YOUR OWN WORLDVIEW

Just like we discussed earlier, the starting place is the teacher's own worldview. A math teacher will need to spend considerable time exploring how the macro-propositions of a biblical worldview live, move, and have their being in the field of math, in the form of math-related micro-propositions. How do those big answers to the biggest of all human questions find their way into a biblical view of math as one small slice of God's grand creation? Remember, this is not an instantaneous occurrence. A deep understanding of God's perspective on math develops over time, just like any other area of knowledge.

> Being that all excellent teachers are lifelong learners, this process of collecting truth claims never has to stop.

But when it comes to the classroom experience, math teachers need to intentionally take time to transmit these micro-propositions to their students, giving them ample opportunities to process these truths through reflection, discussion, and other activities. Doing so may not be in the curriculum, and we may not be able to draw a direct line from learning a micro-proposition to a question on the SAT or the ACT. But if we provide an immersive biblical worldview experience, this cannot be skipped over in favor of more immediate or practical concerns.

1. Collecting Truths

The first step in being able to communicate these truths to students is to collect them. I understand that most classroom teachers have precious little time to find and assemble a comprehensive list of biblical truth claims that relate to their subject area. However, given that the modern biblical worldview movement is maturing, others have assembled such lists, and those resources should be used to the fullest. Math teachers should keep an informal running list of truth claims related to math found in articles, blog posts, books, and other resources. I'm not suggesting that the list needs to be perfectly formatted or even listed on paper. It could merely be a few books or printed articles with significant underlining. Or it could be a collection of index cards with notes written on them. The method or means of collection is not important. What is important is that, over time, math teachers will have compiled a list of dozens of truth claims related to math that can be used with their students. And being that all excellent teachers are lifelong learners, this process of collecting truth claims never has to stop.

As truth claims are collected, these can become springboards for classroom statements and activities. They can also be used in classroom décor and on bulletin boards. Let's think back to our sample truth claim about doing good things dependent on math. The teacher could invite the students to brainstorm all the ways of doing good they can in a three-minute time frame. Then the teacher could lead a discussion encouraging the students to identify which ways of doing good have some relationship to math. They may have to do some digging, but given the pervasive nature of math, students will likely connect it to many of the good things they would like to do in the world. Even a short discussion one day a week that looks something like this would help students nurture a biblical view of math. But there's more fruit that can come from a math teacher collecting and considering micro-propositions that relate to math. And that fruit involves some more spontaneous applications of God's view on math.

> Jesus clearly told us that what we say is a reflection of what is in our hearts; our hearts overflow into our words.

2. Meditating on Truths

Jesus clearly told us that what we say is a reflection of what is in our hearts; our hearts overflow into our words. Given this truth, we can expect the more math teachers meditate on micro-propositions connected with math, the more they will naturally *say* things that reflect what they meditate on. This points to the ultimate way in which a teacher can help students explore God's view of math—through the everyday, spontaneous words a teacher uses in explaining math concepts. But this only happens as the teacher's truth claim reservoir becomes abundantly full to overflowing through regular and bountiful deposits.

If you're new to the ideas I'm suggesting, you can begin simply by compiling a list of micro-propositions related to your subject area. In this, you will be walking in the worthy footsteps of the teacher in Ecclesiastes, who "pondered and searched out and set in order many proverbs" (Ecclesiastes 12:9 NIV). In other words, you should seek out, meditate on, and arrange truth claims related to your field that emerge from the macro-propositions of Scripture.

3. Incorporating Truths with Authenticity

I'm not suggesting that every math concept you teach will have a specific correlating Bible verse. To approach your subject in this manner would most certainly lend an artificial, forced feel. What I'm suggesting is a holistic process in which teachers make it a life endeavor to explore the biblical themes that can inform how Christian teachers should view their area of study.

To help you get started, I'll list some suggested micro-propositions for a few major subject areas:[14]

Literature/English/Language Arts:

- God created storytelling as a method of communicating truth (Eckel, 2003).
- God reveals himself in words; becoming skillful with words enables us to more deeply experience God's revelation and share it with others.
- Studying the etymology and meaning of the words we use is a way to mark the passage of time and to understand how ideas influence human culture.
- In stories, the battle between good and evil is a reflection and result of human sin (Eckel, 2003).
- The forms of poetry and prose reflect the rhythm of reality, speaking profoundly to our very being.
- Literature can reveal the inner workings of a human's soul like perhaps no other medium.
- The ability to use words and symbols to communicate is unique to humans as image-bearers.

- The form and structure of language reflects the orderliness of God and allows human beings to share meaning.
- Words must be stewarded well in order to accurately communicate the truth about the way things really are.
- "Excellence in communication skills is a means of revealing God's character to other people" (Overman and Johnson, 2003, p. 68).

Math:
- The precision, accuracy, and exactitude of measurement are rooted in God's perfection (Eckel, 2003).
- Mathematical patterns are predictable and reliable because a faithful, dependable God established them (Eckel, 2003).
- Arithmetic enables us to account for reality that manifests through the passage of time.
- Geometry enables us to account for reality that manifests through physical space.
- Mathematics is a language God has enabled us to discover, through which we can understand and marvel at God's invisible nature and the universe he has created.
- The structure and function of every facet of the universe is dependent upon the reliability of mathematical truth.
- Mathematical principles provide evidence of a Creator/Designer of the Universe (Overman and Johnson, 2003).
- Human beings can employ math to exert good and godly rulership over creation.
- Math requires precision, self-discipline, and patience. These qualities can be cultivated in humans through humble dependence on God and his Spirit.

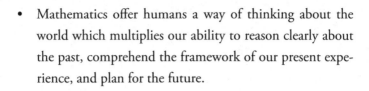

- Mathematics offer humans a way of thinking about the world which multiplies our ability to reason clearly about the past, comprehend the framework of our present experience, and plan for the future.

Science:
- "God is the sovereign Lord, Creator and Sustainer of all things that exist" (Eckel, 2003, p. 154).
- God gave man responsibility to rule over the animals and to develop, cultivate, and protect the earth (Eckel, 2003). This is commonly called the "Creation Mandate."
- Science can be used to create and cultivate flourishing cultures.
- God has revealed his eternal power and divine nature through creation (Romans 1:20). Therefore, human beings can learn about God through close exploration of nature.
- All scientific theories (explanatory models for the way things work) are based on assumptions.
- Scientific principles enable human beings to cure what is broken in cultures, organizations, and individuals.
- A biblical worldview provides reliable and consistent underlying assumptions about the way things truly are, without which science would not be possible (Myers and Noebel, 2015).
- Nature follows established laws, evidencing a rational, purposeful designer (Pearcey and Thaxton, 1994).
- The Biblical worldview provides motives for scientific inquiry: to show God's glory and to explore the wisdom of the Creator (Pearcy and Thaxton, 1994).

History:

- History has a purpose and an end designed and decreed by God (Eckel, 2003).
- History is linear: it is going someplace, and it is going there on purpose (Finn, 2015).
- God established where all people throughout all time were to live.
- History is essentially the record of man's interactions with God and his purposes.
- The forces that come to bear upon human societies are not random, chance forces.
- Recorded history is reflective of man's efforts to document human experience. However, there is only one truly accurate representation for every event in history. Two (differing) representations of a past event cannot both be simultaneously true.
- "God governs the rise and fall of governmental leaders" (Overman and Johnson, 2003, p. 67).
- Reflection on history enables us to be wise so we can stand against the manipulation and deceit of false worldviews.

Fine Arts:

- "Color, form, texture, and sound are part of God's creation, and testify to God's existence and creative/artistic aspects" (Overman & Johnson, 2003, p. 69).
- "As with all aspects of mankind, communication through art and music is subject to God's standards of conduct" (Overman & Johnson, 2003, p. 70).
- Beauty is objective and based on the beauty and excellence of God's good creation.

- Beauty opens our hearts to virtue, inspiring justice and reflection.
- Art can be considered a worshipful response to God's revelation of who he is.
- When humans create art, they are expressing an important element of the image of God in them.
- Artistic expressions need not be overtly "Christian" in their content in order to glorify God and reflect his excellence.
- Music is fundamentally mathematical, with a form and structure that relates to reality itself.

Athletics:

- Human beings should care for their bodies as the dwelling place of the Holy Spirit.
- Athletes should strive for excellence, to the glory of God.
- Mediocrity in sport is often born of laziness, apathy, or rebellion and reflects poorly on God.
- Athletics is an ideal forum in which to nurture the development of Christ-like character in students.

- Sports ideally expose students to many of the elements of real life: teamwork, setbacks, victory, following nonnegotiable rules, submitting to authority, etc. This exposure can help to prepare students for life after high school.
- Athletics is perhaps the most significant connecting point between body and spirit in our culture.

These are just a few examples of the micro-propositions that apply to the various academic disciplines and areas of study. A lifetime commitment to seek out, meditate on, and arrange such truth claims is a key prerequisite for being able to pass on those truth claims to students. Passing on and interacting with those truth claims in the classroom is, as we saw in the example I gave earlier, an intentional, planned teaching/learning activity. However, it is also a spontaneous action as well. This is where we can see the tremendous value of a full micro-proposition reservoir. The imagery that comes to my mind is of entering each class period with a glass of water filled to the brim. As you walk around the classroom, you'll inevitably get knocked and jostled a bit and, as you do, water will spill out. It is the same with

teachers who are brimming with biblical truth claims related to their subject area—those truth claims will spill out all over.

One of the places I see this in action effectively is in one of my favorite podcasts, *The Briefing* by Dr. Albert Mohler. In this half-hour podcast, Mohler teaches on a wide array of subjects that relate to some of the more intense cultural battles occurring today. While he will occasionally take a direct approach in explaining a macro-proposition, he most often seamlessly weaves micro-propositions into everything he says. It's so seamless, in fact, that it can be hard to decipher his transitions. Mohler simply talks in a way that naturally makes connections between current issues and events and how Christians should view those issues and events. What follows is a specific example of Mohler's way of making natural and seamless connections between teaching content and a biblical worldview. In one of his podcasts, he teaches about the current reports of climate change. Prior to this section, he explained some reports about actual, verifiable changes in the environment, including statistics about decreased bird populations and other issues. Let's "listen in" to a master teacher:

> Christians looking at these kinds of reports understand that human beings bear a very important ecological responsibility, not because we are merely the inhabitants of a planet that needs our care and concern, but because we start with a biblical worldview that starts with the biblical doctrine of creation and also understands human beings to be assigned the kind of important responsibility for the environment, for the world, for its use, and for its stewardship.
>
> We understand that that's where our worldview begins. We also come to understand that the biblical

worldview makes very clear that human beings are not a blight upon creation. Whatever problems that we face in that climate and in the environment, the problem is not that human beings exist. The problem is not even that greater numbers of human beings exist. The problem is that we have often not been very thoughtful in understanding the kind of cause and consequence argument that is now being played out in much of the environment.

This is easy to understand in a local scale. It's easy to understand in your own lawn or in your own neighborhood. Decisions made about whether or not to plant vegetation, decisions about cutting down shrubbery, decisions about pavement rather than grass, decisions about what kinds of trees will be existing in the neighborhood, decisions about what kind of lights will be on at night. All of this has an effect upon the environment. That's just one neighborhood. The human beings in that environment also have a stewardship responsibility.

You would hope that that stewardship responsibility would mean that all the neighbors together, just in that one little neighborhood, perhaps in one little square or street, would be careful about the disposal of waste, would be careful about creating too much waste, would be careful about any number of issues. Notice this, we wouldn't be talking about the square and we wouldn't be talking about the street if human beings had not exercised the dominion that is assigned to human beings in Genesis 1. (Mohler, 2019)

I hope you can see in this short passage a fine example of spontaneous and seamless immersion of a subject matter with a biblical worldview. Notice that he's not directly teaching the macro-propositions that relate to care of creation. Rather, in a conversational way, he simply talks about important issues in the context of an applied biblical worldview. This is without any feeling on our part that he's preaching or trying to harness a current issue to artificially make a biblical point.[15]

Throughout my experience in Christian school leadership, I've seen few teachers who do this naturally and easily. I know the teachers who do so have a steady diet of biblical worldview oriented, subject-specific content so that their reservoirs are full to overflowing. In one history class I visited, the teacher discussed with his seventh graders the topic of human migrations throughout history

using a non-Christian textbook. The students were exposed to the various reasons for mass migrations over human history—drought, conquest, trade, and so on. But the textbook offered no suggestion that God's providential workings in history are the prime factor in human migrations. This teacher very naturally wove that truth into the class discussion, pointing to the mass migrations of the people of Israel that took place before and after the Egyptian captivity. He prompted the students to think through why God's people migrated during that time in history. They arrived at a good understanding of God's providence in the story of Israel. He challenged them to apply that knowledge to consider the fuller meaning of other human migrations. It was not preachy or contrived. It was an easy weaving together of an important topic in history with God's view on mass migrations and an understanding of his involvement in that topic. Students left that class with an understanding of human migrations deeply connected to a biblical worldview. And that connection happened as a result of a teacher's full reservoir.

> Situating classroom content within the biblical narrative grounds everything you study in God's overarching plan for humanity.

Unfortunately, some of the most seasoned and effective Christian teachers can miss opportunities like this as a result of not having a steady diet of biblical truth claims and worldview analysis related to their subject area. Once I was looking closely at a school's secular science curriculum to find areas in which the authors subtly undermined a biblical worldview. In the section on biological adaptations, the text explained how ducks enjoy the benefits of an evolutionary adaptation that produces an oily substance for their feathers, causing their feathers to shed water instead of being saturated. Obviously, there was no mention of design—just the blind natural force of adaptation.

This one truth claim—nature provides ducks an adaptation that keeps them from being saturated by water and consequently unable to fly—will likely not deconstruct fourth graders' growing faith in Christ. But a steady, long-term diet of such truth claims that evade the possibility of design essentially inoculates them against the "virus" of false or inaccurate truth claims. Science teachers seeking out truths consistent with Scripture, deeply considering those truths, and arranging them in a way that makes sense will be all the more likely to identify false or inaccurate claims. They will be able to naturally offer satisfying answers for the questions such truth claims suggest. The key is in the seeking, pondering, and arranging that the teacher in Ecclesiastes is famous for having done.

SITUATING TOPICS IN THE BIBLICAL NARRATIVE

Another way to incorporate biblical worldview truths into your classroom is to lead your students to situate all topics in the biblical narrative of *Creation, Fall, Redemption,* and *Restoration.* All of creation and human experience falls somewhere along the continuum between *ought (creation)* and *will (restoration).* So everything you study in your classroom also falls along that continuum. Situating classroom content within the biblical narrative grounds everything you study in God's overarching plan for humanity.

Context is everything. As my college hermeneutics professor drilled into my brain, words only have meaning in context. The same is true of every topic we study. We can gain a certain level of understanding about a topic if we look only at that topic. But we will only grasp its fuller meaning if we see it in a broader context. This is how everyone interprets all aspects of reality. They put them into the broader context of the overarching narrative they've chosen to believe is the most accurate reflection of reality. So secularists situate every problem of mankind into a strictly natural context. Not surprisingly, every solution they devise will be a natural solution.

Marxists look at the woes of the world through a lens that colors everything in relation to the strong oppressing the weak or the rich oppressing the poor. Muslims will perceive everything as either in or out of submission to Allah. Postmodernists look at every truth claim as suspect and every situation as open to multiple interpretations and meanings.

A primary learning task for Christian students is to gain the insight necessary to see how each topic of study relates to the biblical framework of God's redemptive plan. Teachers will need to guide the acquisition of this insight, regularly referring to the *ought, is, can,* and *will* framework.

History is likely the easiest subject to relate to the framework, given that the framework doubles as a universal timeline. However, digging deeper into world events and biographies will give ample opportunity for students to grapple with where exactly those points and eras in history fall on the framework. For example, take Christopher Columbus's mission to find a water passage to India and his accidental discovery of the New World. Elements of this fascinating account fall into multiple sections of the framework. Columbus's indomitable drive to discover a passageway for trade relates to God's creation mandate and represents mankind stewarding his creation and creating conditions that lend towards human flourishing. However, the exploitation of indigenous peoples and natural resources in the Americas made possible by Columbus's discovery is a prime example of how man's selfish nature deeply reflects the

> The very existence of consistent mathematical principles is evidence of God's good, well-ordered creation and is a "means whereby we can think God's thoughts after him" (Rushdoony, 1981, p. 58).

fall of mankind in Adam. Ironically though, the open passageway also made possible the spread of the gospel to people who previously had no witness among them, bringing redemption to entire regions of the globe. Finally, both the positive and negative results of Columbus's life work point to the ultimate restoration of all things. Positively, many humans will experience the joy of heaven because of the missionary endeavors that were made possible by Columbus's bold travels. And the negative impact of Columbus's legacy reminds us that all creation groans, waiting for the final day when all will be made new.

If history is the subject most readily placed in the framework, math is likely the one that requires the most thought to find specific connections. However, doing so is worth the effort. The very existence of consistent mathematical principles is evidence of God's good, well-ordered creation and is a "means whereby we can think God's thoughts after him" (Rushdoony, 1981, p. 58). The fall of man shows up in man's tendency to use the truth of math for less-than-noble ends, such as when investors are defrauded through mathematical sleight of hand. Consumers are often entrapped in the hard mathematical realities of compounding interest on credit cards they never pay off. At a deeper, more philosophical level, mankind has perpetuated offense upon offense toward God by not acknowledging him as the source of all wisdom, including mathematical wisdom.

The spirit of redemption is in action when math is harnessed to serve and bless others. The final restoration of all things will likely include the eternal enjoyment of math throughout all the ages. Humans will be able to explore the depths of the beauty of God's glory as revealed in math without the typical barriers that characterize a selfish and lazy flesh.

The danger here is in making these connections in a trite, superficial, or condescending manner. I'm not talking about slathering your "real" classroom content with a few biblical truths, like spreading a thin veneer of watery paint on a piece of furniture. Situating topics in the biblical narrative framework is part of what Dr. Bryan Smith (n.d.) calls the deepest level of biblical integration—rebuilding academic disciplines with a biblical worldview. Dr. Smith identifies two steps in this process: (1) questioning assumptions and (2) rebuilding the subject from a biblical worldview.

> Questioning assumptions is a great discipline for connecting topics to the biblical narrative framework.

Questioning assumptions is a great discipline for connecting topics to the biblical narrative framework. The truth reflected in all topics of study rest on certain assumptions about why things are the way they are. Good questions can help uncover those assumptions (macro- and micro-propositions). Effective questions can involve the widest breadth of human reasoning:

- "How can we know _____ is true?"
- "How can we know anything is true?"
- "How does the fall of man impact our ability to know anything at all?"

On the other end of the spectrum, questions can unearth the assumptions that support specific ideas and truth claims in the academic subjects:

- Where did Columbus develop his assumptions about the size of the Atlantic Ocean?

- On what fundamental assumptions do all geometric proofs rest?
- Identify the assumptions that secular scientists bring to their work of examining and interpreting the fossil record.
- What assumptions about communication do we need to bring to our study of grammar?

As we lead students to question base assumptions, we help them to think deeply about the narrative frameworks that people hold to be true and that undergird all topics and ideas. Those assumptions, then, can be evaluated in light of the biblical narrative framework. Accurate truth claims reflect creation or redemption, or they prefigure the final restoration of all things. Inaccurate truth claims reflect some aspect of the fall.

> We are ultimately seeking to rebuild our relationship to the various academic subjects with awareness of how God views those areas.

However, we're not questioning assumptions simply to classify topics or ideas in one or another facet of the biblical narrative framework. We are ultimately seeking to rebuild our relationship to the various academic subjects with awareness of how God views those areas. This clarifies what those areas have to teach us about God, his ways, and his character. So we examine and evaluate the assumptions behind the Pythagorean theorem or any other topic. Then we are ready to build our understanding of it in light of whether those assumptions are biblically accurate and where they fit on the framework.

HAVING AN APPLIED BIBLICAL WORLDVIEW

Finally, we need to remember that we don't study our subject areas from a worldview perspective merely to make sure we're thinking properly, though that is obviously an important goal. We also examine all life through the lens of a biblical worldview so we can discover how to practically apply it in our behavior. For this reason, I like the phrase *applied biblical worldview*. This suggests there's more than just knowing and being able to repeat on an assessment the various truth claims that make up the cognitive or propositional nature of a biblical worldview.

The four worldview questions we discussed earlier form an ideal framework within which to consider how a biblical worldview transforms people and situations. Every subject area and every topic within those subject areas can be matched to one of these questions, and often on multiple levels. By way of reminder, those questions are as follows:

- What is good that I can *cultivate*?
- What is missing that I can *create*?
- What is evil that I can *curb*?
- What is broken that I can *cure*?

In literature, stories can be evaluated according to these questions. For any story, you can ask, "What is good, missing, evil, and broken in this story? How do the characters *cultivate, create, curb,* or *cure* in response to those situations?"

For science, you can ask, "How might you use what we've learned in this unit to create something good that is missing in our world?" You can also highlight people who have used science to *cultivate, create, curb,* or *cure*.

In the arts, you can identify and celebrate the reality that your students are actually cultivating good and creating new works of art for the glory of God. They are adding something of beauty where once there were only the raw materials of a musical instrument and a score, or colored pencils and a sheet of paper.

Your study of history can feature a primary focus on evaluating every event and era you study with these four questions.

> Everything can be tied to these questions. They serve not only to help consider how to apply a biblical worldview but to help unify your students' entire experience in school.

In Latin, you can acknowledge the beauty of language as the way our thoughts and ideas are expressed (the way we *create* meaning). Learning to use a different language opens up entire worlds of possibilities for us to *create, cultivate, cure,* and *curb,* because we've *created* a new competency in ourselves.

I hope you can see how everything can be tied to these questions. They serve not only to help consider how to apply a biblical worldview but to help unify your students' entire experience in school.

Being able to do what I'm suggesting here requires that your students deeply understand the four questions. So you'll need to consistently talk about what they mean and how your students can apply them in their daily lives as students. Aim for creating a seamless experience for your students. They begin by cultivating good in the hallways through affirming their friends when they do what is good. Then they create good friendships throughout the year. And then they consider how their new math skills can be harnessed for curing what's broken.

The language of these questions can become *the way* you talk with your students about their God-given responsibility to respond to all of life. You use that same language in reference to everything, from the reason we pick up trash in the hallways to the reason we study genetics so that someday we may discover an important solution for a sickness. Then your students can begin to see all of life as one unified whole, as opposed to the bits and pieces that Francis Schaeffer famously wrote about (Schaeffer, 1981). The way we talk in our *pedagogium* is an important way we shape our students and nurture the development of their worldview.

CHAPTER 12

LEADING THE BIBLICAL WORLDVIEW REVOLUTION

The previous chapters have been addressed primarily to teachers. But if you are an educational leader, I trust you have derived value from what you have read. I also hope you have been challenged to develop your own worldview. But we're not done yet. This chapter is for you as a leader. It describes the final element of a school that faithfully cultivates a biblical worldview immersion experience for our students. What has been laid out in the previous chapters describes schools whose leadership is actively equipping and expecting teachers to do these things.

Right at the outset, I need to say something that is likely already obvious to you. Everything I've written for teachers applies to you too. You must deeply understand what a biblical worldview is. You need to understand how a biblical worldview develops in others, and you must be developing your own worldview. Finally, you need to be living out the same teaching commitments that you want to see in your teachers and other staff members. If you don't live out these ideals in your own leadership and in your teaching/equipping efforts, your school's transformation into an immersive biblical worldview environment will be stymied. In short, you need to *be* what you want the rest of your team to *become*.

> Your teachers need you as a leader to do some things that are well beyond the scope and responsibility of the classroom teacher.

However, I'm not going to leave you here with a vague sense of needing to simply set a good example, though doing so is the essential starting place for leaders. In addition, there are action steps you can take to nurture an environment that immerses students in biblical worldview in every aspect of their school experience. This goes beyond what happens in the classroom, involving initiatives and ideas that are too broad for individual teachers to apply. Your teachers need *you* as a leader to do some things that are well beyond the scope and responsibility of the classroom teacher. For your teachers, I've recommended significant and potentially challenging action steps. They will need you to support them by creating a school-wide *pedagogium* consistent with what they'll be doing in their classrooms.

EXPECTED STUDENT OUTCOMES

Your end view is the place to start your efforts at creating a school-wide environment that functions like a greenhouse for biblical worldview development. What do you want your students to be like when they graduate? What's the profile of your ideal graduate? You can't shape an environment to nurture what you want to see in your graduates if you don't first articulate what you actually hope to see in them.

You likely already have some level of expected student outcomes in mind or on paper. These may relate to biblical worldview development, or they may relate only to academic outcomes. For the purposes of creating a school-wide *pedagogium*, you'll need to evaluate what you have, looking specifically for those expected student outcomes that relate directly to biblical worldview development.

Back in chapter 5 I gave a sample list of expected student outcomes based on the research I conducted with emerging adults. This list is reproduced here and can be a starting place for your work in refining your school's vision of what kind of student you want to produce. Of course, your school needs expected student outcomes that relate to all the academic areas as well. This list only articulates outcomes related to biblical worldview development.

Sample List of Expected Student Outcomes

By the time our students graduate, they will

- be aware of their own worldview;
- be committed to actively processing new life experiences in meaningful ways;
- own the ongoing development of their worldview;
- identify the impact that various childhood experiences have had on their worldview;
- have had multiple meaningful interactions with individuals who espouse various non-Christian worldviews;
- have had significant practice in processing new experiences through peer discussions, reflection, study, and prayer;

- have had at least one significant mentoring relationship with an individual who has a well-developed biblical worldview;
- have served in at least one teaching or mentoring context that provided the opportunity to serve individuals whose worldview is less developed;
- have participated in a minimum of one formal worldview course on the high school or college level;
- have learned effective strategies to manage stress, especially academic pressures, relationship challenges, and the expectations of others;
- have learned effective strategies to manage distractions, such as social media, entertainment, and so on; and
- have embraced a biblical view of trials and difficulties and have demonstrated success in navigating those trials and difficulties.

I know this can seem like an ambitious list. However, if we are serious about biblical worldview development, we need to think clearly about what we're aiming for in our students. I hope you notice in this list that I have purposefully not described a fully mature biblical worldview. Remember, high school graduates are still very much in process. My research suggests that having a strong, well-developed biblical worldview comes

> In addition to taking academic classes that are biblical worldview aligned, students also need courses designed specifically to explore a biblical worldview.

several years after graduation and the process of strengthening one's worldview continues throughout all of life.

After developing a research-based list of outcomes you desire to see in your students, you then work backward through their time in school to craft experiences that will lead them to demonstrate those outcomes. One experience is the actual classes you require your students to take. In my research project, I found that all but just a small handful of my study participants had to take biblical worldview classes in their K–12 school experience. Those who did not reported having to do significant "catch-up" work in college and after college to fill out their understanding of a biblical worldview. In addition to taking academic classes that are biblical worldview aligned, students also need courses designed specifically to explore a biblical worldview.

COURSES AND CLASSES

The most obvious department of the school to include such courses is the Bible department. Bible classes all the way down to your school's youngest learners can be designed to incrementally build cognitive understanding of a biblical worldview. Start with evaluating what you already do by laying out your entire Bible scope and sequence to see how your school gives age-appropriate focus to a biblical worldview. Be sure to look at everything from pre-K to twelfth grade. Sometimes schools evaluate their curriculum in divisional silos, which tends toward a disjointed curricular experience for your students. The ideal is that, year after year, your students are mastering the content of a biblical worldview and experiencing seamless support for worldview development.

After you lay out your scope and sequence, you'll likely need to also review the curricular resources your teachers use. This will help you get a more complete picture of how your school approaches biblical worldview across the full spectrum of grades. Already, you may be seeing some deficiencies in the list of expected student outcomes I provided above. I approached that list as a basis for assessing your school's overall approach to biblical worldview development. However, there is nothing in that list about understanding the basic tenets of a biblical worldview, perceiving the Bible as a whole, or comparing and contrasting a biblical worldview with other competing worldviews. Ideally, the curricular materials you give to your teachers contain sets of student outcomes or learning objectives at each grade level. When aggregated together, they provide a comprehensive list of outcomes for your school's specific biblical worldview related courses.

> All biblical studies, whether the life of Christ or OT history, should all include the expectation that students will gain additional raw materials they can fit into the larger framework of a biblical worldview.

In general, I suggest that studies in biblical worldview cannot start too early. Even with your youngest learners, you can and should lay a good foundation for understanding of all of life through the lens of a biblical worldview. We do not have space to evaluate all the Bible curricula choices you have. But I encourage you to think carefully about how your school lays out your Bible curriculum incrementally, year after year, to build a solid worldview understanding in your students. All biblical studies, whether the life of Christ or OT history, should include the expectation that students will gain additional raw materials they can fit into the larger framework of a biblical worldview.

In the later grades, it is appropriate to expect students to devote a semester or an entire year to an in-depth study of a biblical worldview. Additionally, with what we learned from the young adults in my study, another course in comparative worldviews would be extremely helpful. You certainly wouldn't want a graduate from your school to walk into a secular university classroom to be confronted by a Marxist professor without having studied some of what a modern Marxist believes and teaches.

CURRICULAR CHOICES

Beyond courses designed to focus exclusively on biblical worldview, it is important to evaluate all your curricular materials. I hope by now you've picked up on my concerns about the ability that many teachers have in approaching their subject matter from a biblical worldview perspective. A reasonable assumption we can make about our teachers is that they need significant curricular support to do so. This is a strong apologetic for providing curricular materials that do some of the heavy lifting for our teachers. These curricula make those connections for them and suggest other resources that can be used to help our students rebuild math or science or language arts from a biblical perspective.

Recently, I had a discussion with an elementary teacher in a school that recently adopted three new elementary curricula in several subject areas. This teacher was one of those exceptional teachers who is deeply conversant with a biblical worldview and is actively engaged in developing her own worldview. She's already doing much of what I've recommended in this book.

> Christian curriculum is helping her create a unified and holistic *pedagogium* for her class.

However, in our conversation, she highlighted the invaluable support that a Christian-written curriculum is for her in the classroom.

Besides assisting her to make connections in each academic discipline alone, she remarked that the support from the curricula helps to make connections *across* the disciplines. Christian curriculum is helping her create a unified and holistic *pedagogium* for her class.

I know this idea can spark heated emotions among Christian school leaders and teachers. Some believe Christian curricula are not on par academically with secular materials. Others believe students need to get more than the Christian party line and need to be exposed to other thinking. However, I'm not sure most Christian schoolteachers have the know-how and experience to immerse their subject areas in a biblical worldview without the support that curricular materials written specifically for that purpose can provide. It is possible to do the research necessary to do so, but I don't know many K–12 teachers who have the time available that's needed for that level of preparation.

The other issue is that secular curricula (written for the secularist worldview immersed public schools) is full of subtleties that are inconsistent with a biblical worldview. In addition to the duck feathers example I mentioned earlier, here are two examples of subtle inconsistencies I have recently discovered.

First, our school library has traditionally used the Scholastic current events papers in our elementary classes. Not long ago, I was curious about what the current paper contained. Its feature article celebrated the many women elected to serve in Congress in the midterm election of 2018. It was a fair treatment of the accomplishments of women in the US, an idea worthy of our students' attention.

However, as the article closed, it pointed to the "fact" that the US Declaration of Independence, while the basis for the new opportunities that women now enjoy, does not specifically

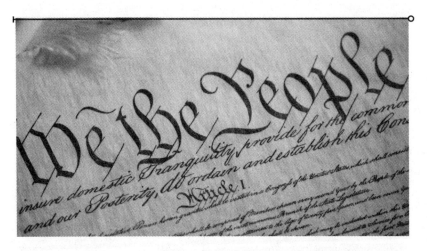

mention women. Instead, the article said, it only mentions men. To provide evidence for this point, it quoted the following line from the Declaration: "All men are created equal." The accompanying commentary said nothing about how the words *men, mankind,* and related words were used at the time of the writing of the Declaration of Independence to refer to both sexes. Instead, the author implied that women were purposefully *excluded* from the statement about all men being created equal. A quick look in the Oxford English Dictionary, which documents the meaning of English words over time, makes it abundantly clear that the word *men* in this context and era would most certainly have meant men *and* women.

While I'm not saying that twisting the meaning of one word is a frontal assault on a Christian worldview, it certainly reflects an overall bias against being careful to find the truth in how words are used. More specifically, it provides evidence of either an overt twisting of truth to serve a particular agenda or a careless disregard for truth. In either scenario, the seeds planted in young minds can bear antibiblical worldview thoughts later. And think about how attentive the teacher would need to be to catch something like this in the midst of reading with a bunch of first graders!

My other example is similar. A second-grade language text included commentary on the Pledge of Allegiance, leading the teacher

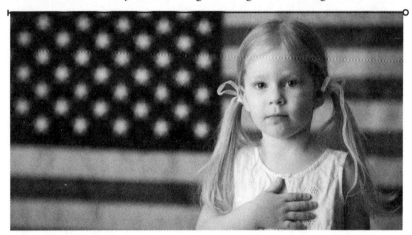

to help students grasp the meaning of each phrase. The commentary that the teacher was to share with the students went right from a few comments on *one nation* to an explanation of the word *indivisible*. Notice anything missing there? While *under God* was printed in the text, the teacher guide completely ignored that phrase as if it didn't exist. Don't get me wrong—I'm not saying that you need to recite the whole Pledge of Allegiance if you're a *real* Christian. Not at all. What I am pointing to is the reality that a text written for a secularism-saturated school system is inadequate for use in a school that intends to immerse students in a biblical worldview. Remember what secularism states—God is irrelevant. And this simple example shows how one textbook handled the inconvenient mention of God in the Pledge—it simply ignored it. This is consistent with the big-picture agenda of secularism—ignore God, and maybe he'll eventually go away.

As these few examples demonstrate, the subtleties of the belief systems of non-Christian authors will permeate their work, just as the Christian worldview ought to permeate the work of Christians. This reminds me of C. S. Lewis's important book, *The Abolition of Man* (1974), which many consider to be the key to all his other writings. The first line of this towering work is "I doubt whether we are sufficiently attentive to the importance of elementary textbooks" (Lewis, 1974, p. 1). Lewis goes on to critique an English textbook designed to be used in school by boys and girls across the United Kingdom—children whose minds and hearts were being shaped in school. Lewis argues that the underlying values and assumptions in the text are as important as the specific content the text was meant to transmit. As I noted earlier, we as teachers can often miss those assumptions, though they powerfully shape the hearts and minds of students.

The text Lewis evaluated subtly promoted the philosophy of relativism, clearly seen in the questions it asked regarding a particular story. Relativism (which is closely related to postmodernism) is a way of thinking in which there is no room for fixed reference points. Instead, every reality is subject to the ideas and thoughts of the observer. Lewis acknowledged that no elementary student

> The underlying values and assumptions in the text are as important as the specific content the text was meant to transmit.

would read those questions and say, "By golly, relativism is the way to go!" However, the seeds of relativism sown by those questions will bear fruit long into the future. He explains,

> The very power of [the textbook writers] depends on the fact that they are dealing with a boy: a boy who thinks he is doing his "English prep" and has no notion that ethics, theology, and politics are at stake. It is not a theory they put into his mind, but an assumption, which ten years later, its origin forgotten and its presence unconscious, will condition him to take one side in a controversy which he has never recognized as a controversy at all. (Lewis, 1974, p. 5)

He goes on to suggest that the authors likely do not know what they're doing, and I agree—to an extent. I don't imagine that most textbook authors are sitting in some smoke-filled room conspiring to change the values and assumptions of our students. But they are writing out of their worldviews—they can't help it. And as they do, they include facts, truths, illustrations, questions, and so on that emerge naturally from their worldview.

As a Christian school leader, you must evaluate the materials your school uses to discern what they are promoting. If they are promoting a secular worldview, then you have a decision to make. Either consider investing in new textbooks or equip your teachers to identify and refute the overt *and* subtle statements that contradict a biblical worldview.

HELPING STUDENTS MANAGE DERAILERS

If you think back to my research with young adults, you'll recall there's something else we need to consider as we plan our courses. Biblical worldview development can be stymied by derailers—those pesky life issues that can be like monkey wrenches in the system of healthy development. The classes and experiences you offer in school can proactively equip your students to be prepared to manage those challenges. For instance, since stress in general can be a major derailer—and financial stress in particular—you should consider how you can prepare your students to manage their finances well. By requiring a course in biblical stewardship (money management), you're not only teaching an intensely practical life skill, you're heading off future stress that can seriously derail the worldview development process. Other sources of stress can be related to body image, academic pressure, family disfunction, and other issues. An overall approach to equipping students for emotionally healthy living should be a hallmark of Christian schools.

> Trials are a regular feature of everyone's life. Equipping students to process those challenges in a healthy way can be integrated into multiple formats from chapel services to classroom devotionals as well as in the guidance programs.

Other derailers include distractions and trials. These can both be addressed with students of all ages. The young adults in my study cited ubiquitous media distractions as the chief disruption to disciplined and focused living. This issue may not fit neatly into a typical course format. But it can certainly be addressed in chapel and in events designed to equip parents to help their children manage the media monster.

Trials are a regular feature of everyone's life. Equipping students to process those challenges in a healthy way can be integrated into multiple formats from chapel services to classroom devotionals as well as in the guidance programs. Many times these topics are addressed in isolation from the overall mission of the school. But in a biblical worldview immersed school, they can be deeply connected to the expected student outcomes that relate to the school's core purpose.

THE HIDDEN WORLDVIEW CURRICULUM

The outcomes you expect to see in your students should shape more than your decisions related to which courses to offer and curricular materials to use. They should also feature prominently in the informal elements of your students' and families' experience with your school. By informal, I mean the aspects of school life that happen outside of the set curriculum. Others have called this the hidden curriculum. Some examples of your hidden curriculum include your school's physical plant, your communications, and the non-classroom activities and functions of your school.

1. Décor

I understand that most Christian schools do not have significant funds to allocate to making changes or additions to their physical space. However, there are simple things you can do to make your students' physical interactions with your building consistent with a commitment to biblical worldview immersion. The most obvious area is in the décor you have around your building—something you may or may not pay much attention to. It's easy to lose sight of what's on your walls and in your common areas, especially if you've been a leader in your school for a long period of time. This is a good reason to invite someone with an eye for aesthetics and detail to be a "secret shopper" of sorts.

To help you see your building with fresh eyes, invite a trusted colleague from another school to help you see what messages are being communicated around your building. Before this visit, share with your friend the school's mission statement and worldview-related expected student outcomes. Ask the person to carefully review the written materials explaining your mission. As the observer walks around your building, have him or her note all the messages being sent by what can be seen. This would include overt messages, such as bulletin boards and signage, and more subtle messages, such as how the building looks from a cleanliness and upkeep standpoint.

We tend to minimize the impact the physical plant has on what we're seeking to accomplish in the lives of our students. But if much of what they see (and physically experience) is not consistent with what we say is important, we're missing opportunities to provide immersive reminders about what we say is most important. Every bulletin board and wall hanging can be a billboard for aspects of your mission. Just as marketers think carefully about how to craft and present messages, school leaders should consider how to best use the wall space around the school to promote biblical worldview messages.

> Every bulletin board and wall hanging can be a billboard for aspects of your mission.

2. The Learning Environment

Beyond wall hangings and overt messages, you should also consider the more subtle messages your building sends. If you're always talking about the importance of community, but don't provide spaces where students can informally relate, you're sending mixed messages. You can tell your teachers to plan engaging learning activities. But if you do not encourage them to think through creative ways to set up their classrooms and allocate budget money for collaborative workspaces, you set them up for frustration. I recently asked a few high schoolers in an elective class I teach what they would like to change about our school. I expected them to suggest a new technology policy or to complain about our uniform code. But surprisingly, they were most passionate about classroom set-up. They said having the same uncomfortable furniture laid out in the same way in each room makes them feel like they're in prison. Ouch.

> Whether you're emailing a notice about the start of the school year, greeting families and guests at the Christmas concert, or opening the annual Grandparents' Day chapel, take those opportunities to quickly recast vision for biblical worldview development.

3. Communication with Parents

School leaders also have numerous opportunities to impact parents' understanding of a biblical worldview through the many communication pieces they send home. This also happens every time they get up in front of a group of parents. Many times, leaders fall into habits of minimalist communication, giving people just the facts. They forget that people need to have vision recast continuously in order for it to stick. I once heard from some leadership guru that vision needs to be recommunicated at least twenty times a year. I heard that maxim probably twenty-five years ago, when distractions were much fewer than they are today. I'd update his maxim to say that vision needs to be communicated *every chance you get*. Whether you're emailing a notice about the start of the school year, greeting families and guests at the Christmas concert, or opening the annual Grandparents' Day chapel, take those opportunities to quickly recast vision for biblical worldview development. At a concert, you can remind people of God's perspective on beauty in music. In an email you can restate why you're in business. On Facebook you can post regular quotes from Christian thinkers and authors, such as C. S. Lewis, G. K. Chesterton, or Nancy Pearcy. These informal means can be among the most powerful ways to immerse your students and families in a biblical worldview. The goal is that, at every turn, parents and students are reminded of the distinct mission of your school—to help students develop a biblical worldview.

4. Extracurricular Activities

You also have a bevy of opportunities to shape your students' worldview through the numerous extracurricular activities your school plans each year. We can't possibly cover every potential activity in your school in this chapter. Instead, let me offer you a simple question that should become an essential guiding question for everything you do—from planning the homecoming dance to the Fun Run or other fundraisers you do. The question is, "How can this activity immerse our students in a biblical worldview?" You may want to even print this in big letters to be hung in the room where your leadership team meetings occur. Or write it on an index card and post it on your computer monitor. Make it your smartphone background screen. Do whatever you need to do to keep it front and center in all the planning decisions you make. You may infuse new meaning into traditional activities. Alternatively, you may decide that an activity is not worth doing if it can't be leveraged for biblical worldview immersion.

ARTICULATING EXPECTATIONS

Thinking back to what goes on in the classroom, remember that you can't expect what you don't *articulate* and *inspect*. In the context of what we're discussing in this book, if you expect your teachers to provide an immersive biblical worldview experience for your students, you need to clearly explain what that looks like. Then regularly inspect your teachers' work and provide them with feedback on what you see.

In my current school, I worked with a team of teachers to describe what biblical worldview immersion looks like in terms of specific teacher behaviors and characteristics. The following is an adaptation of one section of our "Guide for Excellence in Teaching and Learning." (This is just one guideline for excellence; we have nine others that relate to all areas of a teacher's work.)

The guideline begins with a brief description, which is followed by specific indicators.

Biblical Worldview Immersion

Biblical worldview immersion is a holistic approach to teaching and learning that honors Scripture as the primary shaper of desires, thoughts, and actions, and recognizes that biblical worldview development is a process that will extend long into adulthood.

1.1. Teacher is deeply committed to living out the truth of Scripture in his/her personal life and is actively involved in studying the Bible and nurturing his/her own spiritual growth

1.2. Teacher is aware of his/her worldview and is committed to lifelong worldview development

1.3. Teacher understands the three dimensions of a biblical

worldview (truth propositions; heart inclination; and behavioral alignment), and the three dispositions of worldview development (awareness of worldview; commitment to meaningful processing; and personal ownership of the process of development)

1.4. Teacher articulates a biblical perspective on each subject area/topic which he/she teaches

1.5. Teacher consistently connects classroom activities to the biblical narrative (*ought/is/can/will*)

1.6. Teacher consistently challenges students to consider application of knowledge through the four applied worldview questions (What can I *create/cultivate/curb/cure?*)

1.7. Teacher assesses students' biblical worldview thinking in assignments and assessments

Like many aspects of excellent teaching, elements of this guideline are difficult to observe. For instance, it's hard for an administrator to "see" firsthand if a teacher is aware of his or her worldview (indicator 1.2). However, a robust and holistic teacher-feedback process includes administrator observations; teacher self-reflection; and peer, parent, and student feedback on teacher performance. These indicators can be meaningfully assessed, providing

> The more your teachers immerse themselves in a biblical worldview, the more they will naturally use language that reflects the biblical narrative and the four applied worldview questions.

an overall picture of whether or not a teacher is sustaining the type of *pedagogium* that immerses students in a biblical worldview.

Indicators 1.1 through 1.3 do not easily lend to direct observation, though the *impact* of these practices and qualities can be seen. For these indicators, I rely on teacher self-reflection. In our annual teacher development process, we require teachers to complete a self-assessment project (which is in itself consistent with the worldview development process). As part of their self-reflection, they answer questions related to their personal spiritual growth, including specific actions they took over the course of the year to study the Bible and live out a biblical worldview (indicator 1.1). They also answer questions that probe how aware they are of their own worldview and how they are taking steps to develop it further (indicator 1.2). For instance, a query that coincides with indicator 1.2 might be, "Describe steps you've taken this year to further develop your worldview," or "Explain two to three areas in which your worldview needs further development."

Indicator 1.3 is more difficult to assess, as it relates to a teacher's understanding of what a worldview is and how a worldview develops. At the simplest level, a teacher can be asked to define the term worldview and to describe the three dispositions of a developing worldview. However, this is simply asking for recall and is a lower-level assessment. With new teachers, this may be a good place to start. However, a teacher's expertise in these concepts must go deeper than that. A more challenging query that would provide more insight into a teacher's understanding of these concepts might be, "Identify several specific action steps you have taken in the last year to shape your students' desires to more accurately reflect a biblical worldview. Describe the results or impact of those actions, including how you could improve in the year to come."

Indicators 1.4 through 1.7 can be directly observed, as they describe clear teacher behaviors. For 1.4, you can do classroom observations, watching for overt connections between course content and biblical perspectives on the topics being studied. The same goes for 1.5 and 1.6. The more your teachers immerse themselves in a biblical worldview, the more they will naturally use language that reflects the biblical narrative and the four applied worldview questions. Indicator 1.7 can be inspected by actually looking at assessments and assignments, which will give you a clear portrait of what is important to the teacher. Sometimes teachers can get so focused on what they say and do in front of the class, they minimize the shaping influence of the choices they make about what they require students to produce. Tests, quizzes, assignments, and projects should be marked by biblical worldview immersion, just like class time should.

All of these indicators can also be assessed by looking at your teachers' classrooms and the bulletin boards in the hallways that they're assigned to maintain. Are there overt biblical worldview statements and ideas included in their décor? For elementary teachers, which assignments do they choose to showcase in the hallways? In our school, the elementary wing has a central display case that teachers rotate responsibility for maintaining throughout the year. As we have talked more and more about biblical worldview immersion, it has been satisfying to see that area increasingly reflect biblical worldview concepts. As you observe these positive changes happening, be sure to provide encouraging feedback to your team. And if you're not seeing things change—in or out of the classroom—note that to them as well.

This may seem obvious, but if you want your teachers to demonstrate the indicators above, you as a leader need to do so as well. You have to provide a great example in the broader *pedagogium* you create for the school. This includes the wall hangings in your office, the times you speak in chapel, and the update emails you send to your team.

PROFESSIONAL DEVELOPMENT

In addition to good modeling, though, you must also provide professional development experiences to equip your teachers to do what you're asking them to do. Just as with your students, you can't simply tell your teachers to create a *pedagogium* immersed in a biblical worldview. You need to equip them to do so. This is not a book on professional development, so I can't go into too much detail here. However, I can give you some suggestions.

> Given that worldview development is a lifelong process, as long as your teaching team members are in your school, they'll need your support to develop their worldview.

As a foundation, plan to make the study of a biblical worldview an ongoing expectation. You'll never get to the point where you can kick back in your leadership easy chair with hands folded behind your head and say, "Mission accomplished!" Given that worldview development is a lifelong process, as long as your teaching team members are in your school, they'll need your support to develop their worldview. This support includes direct instruction in a biblical worldview. I've found that high school biblical worldview texts make a great curriculum for teachers. In our weekly employee devotions, I am currently teaching through one such book and doing so is helping me to provide organized and purposeful training for my team.

To multiply my efforts in this, I record my fifteen-minute teachings on my iPhone. I post them on Google Drive and send a link to all employees, including coaches, aides, and others who are not in the building first thing on Tuesday mornings. In this way, every employee is provided with much of what they need to be on the same page. I'm always amazed (and gratified) by the comments related to the recordings that I get from coaches with whom I hardly ever interact because of our different schedules. They express tremendous appreciation for the opportunity to hear about the mission-critical themes and values we consider to be most important at our school.

In addition, I recommend that you devote time at every professional development day to biblical worldview. In a recent PD day with our entire team (pre-K–12), we did an in-depth study of abortion from a biblical perspective. While abortion is most certainly not in most of these teachers' scope and sequences, they need to be challenged to deeply process this and other critical topics. These times of instruction and exploration are not merely about preparing teachers to teach content. They are about fostering the development of your teachers' worldviews. The topics that merit thoughtful, worldview-based exploration are endless. It may well be that your team members are not getting that kind of input and challenge in other settings.

Particular attention should be given to the new teachers on your team each year. Regardless of where they went to school or where they previously taught, it is safe to assume that they need foundational instruction and mentoring in a biblical worldview. We bring our new teachers in before the veterans each year to provide a few days of in-depth orientation. This includes introducing them to the primary biblical worldview concepts we expect everyone to understand. Additionally, I like to meet with them periodically throughout the year to provide extra support to them as they acclimate to the idea of teaching as biblical worldview immersion. Many of these meetings are nothing more than informal conversations about biblical worldview themes in the faculty lounge or a teacher's classroom. I also believe requiring new teachers to read a book on biblical worldview immerses *them* in an environment similar to the one you're expecting them to create for their students. You can also assign them to listen to specific podcasts and other forms of input.

"Everything rises and falls on leadership" (Roberson, 1977). This is as true in the arena of worldview development as it is in every other area of school life. If you're serious about leading your team to fulfill the worldview promises your school makes, you simply have no choice but to make biblical worldview the centerpiece of your leadership and your expectations for your team.

EPILOGUE

We've covered a lot of ground together in this book, but it is just the beginning of an even longer journey. If you commit to fashion a *pedagogium* that immerses your students in a biblical worldview, you'll likely be working on it for the rest of your teaching career. Just as worldview development is a lifelong process, so is the development of your teaching craft. You'll never stop developing as a teacher. And if you do, it's probably time to hang up the whiteboard markers and call it quits.

I have boundless hope for you and for the Christian school movement in general. Many naysayers (from within and without) are highlighting the enormous challenges we face without seeing the hopeful lining behind the ominous clouds. However, the storm we face is forcing us to reevaluate our basic assumptions about why we're in business and to conceive afresh what excellent teaching should look like in a Christian school classroom. Great hope sounds sweetest "in the Gale" (Dickinson, 2019, p. 94).

I see the future as full of promising prospects for the modern Christian school movement. Not since our humble beginnings in the early to mid-1900s have we had such an opportunity to envision our purpose and truly create places where a comprehensive and authentic biblical worldview takes deep root in students' lives. I believe that, as we do, we'll stand out more and more as a shining city on a hill.

In *That Hideous Strength*, C. S. Lewis (1974) describes a grim dystopian future in which people are molded in an institution that functions as a tool of an overbearing state. The institution is a warped think tank called the National Institute of Coordinated Experiments, or NICE for short. NICE is a hypercontrolling entity that promotes the formation of individuals into ideal citizens of the equally controlling state.

But Lewis conceived of a counter institution that is described more like a household (a *pedagogium*) than a school—St. Anne's. In this sanctuary for human flourishing, solitude, life-giving fellowship, and deep thinking are fostered, and individuals who live there are nourished by a truly transcendent vision of the good life. Ultimately, St. Anne's stands in sharp contrast to the mechanistic and dehumanizing education foisted upon people by NICE. The small school on the hill represents the kind of *pedagogium* I've been advocating in this book.

In contemporary society, the controlling, secular educational system (and certainly the philosophy behind that system) has become openly hostile to an education (or a life) drenched in a biblical worldview. And just as St. Anne's shined as a beacon on a hill in *That Hideous Strength*, I pray your classroom and your school will shine brightly and clearly as places where today's students can be formed into young adults who have gained the God-soaked habits, knowledge, and heart orientation they need in order to be truly different in a crooked and warped generation.

"… that you may be blameless and innocent,
children of God without blemish in the midst
of a crooked and wicked generation, among
whom you shine as lights in the world."
Philippians 2:15

BIBLIOGRAPHY

Ash, Sarah and Patti Clayton. 2009. "Generating, Deepening, and Documenting Learning: The Power of Critical Reflection in Applied Learning." *Journal of Applied Learning in Higher Education* 1:25–48.

Colby, Anne, Thomas Ehrlich, Elizabeth Beaumont, and Jason Stephens. 2003. *Educating Citizens: Preparing America's Undergraduates for Lives of Moral and Civic Responsibility.* California: Jossey Bass.

Dewey, John. 1910. *How We Think.* Boston: D.C. Heath & Co.

Dickinson, Emily. 2019. *Hope Is the Thing with Feathers: The Complete Poems of Emily Dickinson.* Utah: Gibbs Smith.

Eckel, Mark. 2003. *The Whole Truth: Classroom Strategies for Biblical Integration.* Florida: Xulon Press.

Eliot, T. S. 1943. *Four Quartets.* New York: Houghton Mifflin Harcourt Publishing.

Finn, Nathan A. 2016. *History: A Student's Guide.* Illinois: Crossway Books.

Heick, Terry. "5 Levels of Student Engagement: A Continuum for Teaching." TeachThought.com. https://www.teachthought.com/pedagogy/levels-of-student-engagement-continuum/ (Accessed December 23, 2019).

Himmele, Persida and William Himmele. 2017. *Total Participation Techniques: Making Every Student an Active Learner* (2nd ed.). Virginia: ASCD.

Kant, Immanuel. 1790/1987. *The Critique of Judgment* (W. Pluhar, Trans.). Indiana: Hackett.

Kaye, Cathryn. 2004. *Complete Guide to Service-Learning: Proven, Practical Ways to Engage Students in Civic Responsibility, Academic Curriculum, and Social Action*. Minnesota: Free Spirit Publishing.

Kruger, Justin and David Dunning. 2000. "Unskilled and Unaware of It: How Difficulties in Recognizing One's Own Incompetence Lead to Inflated Self-Assessments." *Journal of Personality and Social Psychology* 77:1121–34.

Leinenweber, John. 1992. *The Letters of Saint Augustine*. Missouri: Triumph Books.

Lewis, C. S. 1974. *That Hideous Strength: A Modern Fairy-Tale for Grown-Ups*. New York: Scribner.

Lewis, C. S. 1974. *The Abolition of Man*. New York: Harper Collins.

Lockerbie, D. Bruce. 2005. *A Christian Paideia: The Habitual Vision of Greatness*. Colorado: Purposeful Design.

Martindale, Wayne and Jerry Root, Eds. 1990. *The Quotable Lewis*. Illinois: Tyndale House Publishers.

Mohler, Albert. 2019. "Part I—Young People Across the World Participate in Climate Strike: The Christian Responsibility of Stewardship of Creation." Podcast Audio. *The Briefing*. September 23, 2019. https://albertmohler.com/2019/09/23/briefing-9-23-19.

Moreland, James. 2007. *Kingdom Triangle: Recover the Christian Mind, Renovate the Soul, Restore the Spirit's Power*. Michigan: Zondervan.

Myers, Jeff. 2010. *Cultivate: Forming the Emerging Generation Through Life-on-Life Mentoring*. Tennessee: Passing the Baton International.

Myers, Jeff and David Noebel, 2015. *Understanding the Times: A Survey of Competing Worldviews*. Colorado: Summit Ministries.

Naugle, David. 2002. *Worldview: The History of a Concept*. Michigan: Wm. B. Eerdmans.

Overman, Christian and Don Johnson. 2003. *Making the Connections: How to Put Biblical Worldview Integration into Practice*. Washington: The Biblical Worldview Institute.

Oxford English Dictionary. 2nd ed. Oxford: Oxford University Press, 2004.

Parks, Sharon. 1981. *The Critical Years: The Young Adult Search for a Faith to Live By*. California: Harper and Row.

Pearcey, Nancy R. and Charles Thaxton. 1994. *The Soul of Science: Christian Faith and Natural Philosophy*. Illinois: Crossway Books.

Phillips, W. Gary, William Brown, and John Stonestreet. 2008. *Making Sense of Your World: A Biblical Worldview* (2nd ed.). Wisconsin: Sheffield Press.

Piper, John. 2013. *Brothers, We Are Not Professionals: A Plea to Pastors for Radical Ministry*. Tennessee: Broadman and Holman.

Richardson, Will. 2016. "Getting Schools Ready for the World." *Educational Leadership* 74/4: 24–29.

Roberson, Lee. 1977. *Double-Breasted*. Tennessee: Sword of the Lord Publishers.

Rushdoony, Rousas J. 1985. *The Philosophy of the Christian Curriculum*. California: Ross House Books.

Schaeffer, Francis. 1981. *A Christian Manifesto*. Illinois: Crossway Books.

Schaeffer, Francis. 1984. *The Great Evangelical Disaster*. Illinois: Crossway Books.

Schön, Donald. 1983. *The Reflective Practitioner: How Professionals Think in Action*. New York: Basic Books.

Sire, James. 2015. *Naming the Elephant: Worldview as a Concept* (2nd ed.). Illinois: Intervarsity Press.

Smith, Bryan. n.d. "Biblical Integration: Pitfalls and Promise." BJUpress.com. https://www.bjupress.com/images/pdfs/bible-integration.pdf (accessed December 29, 2019).

Smith, David. 2018. *On Christian Teaching: Practicing Faith in the Classroom*. Michigan: W. B. Eerdmans.

Smith, James. 2009. *Desiring the Kingdom: Worship, Worldview, and Cultural Formation*. Michigan: Baker Academic.

Sousa, David. 2003. *How the Brain Learns* (3rd ed.). California: Corwin Press.

Stoner, Thomas. "Teacher Preparation for Distinctive Evangelical Schools." EdD diss., Boston University School of Education, 2012.

Stonestreet, John and Warren Smith. 2015. *Restoring All Things: God's Audacious Plan to Change the World through Everyday People*. Michigan: Baker Books.

Swaner, Lynn and Roger Erdvig. 2018. *Bring It to Life: Christian Education and the Transformative Power of Service-Learning*. Colorado: Association of Christian Schools International.

Van DeMille, Oliver. 2000. *A Thomas Jefferson Education: Teaching a Generation of Leaders for the Twenty-First Century*. Utah: George Wyeth College Press.

Willard, Dallas. 2002. *Renovation of the Heart: Putting on the Character of Christ*. Colorado: NavPress.

Wolterstorff, Nicholas. 1980. *Educating for Responsible Action*. Michigan: Wm. B. Eerdmans.

RECOMMENDED RESOURCES

for Shaping the Worldview of
Christian Schoolteachers and Leaders

Biblical Worldview Podcasts and Other Online Resources
- *The World and Everything in It* — world.wng.org/radio/worldandeverything
- *The Briefing with Albert Mohler Breakpoint* — breakpoint.org
- The Culture Translator (Axis) — axis.org/ct
- Summit's Weekly Reflect Email — summit.org/resources/reflect
- Center for the Advancement of Christian Education — cace.org

YouTube Channels
- The Eric Metaxas Radio Show
- Prager U
- Summit Ministries
- The Bible Project
- Cold Case Christianity with J. Warner Wallace
- Dr. Sean McDowell

General Biblical Worldview

- *Naming the Elephant: Worldview as a Concept* by James Sire
- *Worldview: History of a Concept* by David Naugle
- *Total Truth: Liberating Christianity from Its Cultural Captivity* by Nancy Pearcey
- *Understanding the Times: A Survey of Competing Worldviews* by Jeff Myers and David Noebel
- *The Secret Battle of Ideas about God: Answers to Life's Biggest Questions* by Jeff Myers
- *Making Sense of Your World: A Biblical Worldview* by W. Gary Phillips, William E. Brown, and John Stonestreet
- *How Now Shall We Live?* by Charles Colson and Nancy Pearcey
- *Creation Regained: A Biblical Basis for a Reformational Worldview* by Albert M. Wolters

Biblical Worldview: Heart Orientation

- *Renovation of the Heart: Putting on the Character of Christ* by Dallas Willard
- *Desiring the Kingdom: Worldview, Worship, and Cultural Formation* by James K. A. Smith
- *Reordered Loves, Reordered Lives: Learning the Deep Meaning of Happiness* by David Naugle

Biblical Worldview: Cognitive Dimension

- *Love the Lord with All Your Mind: The Role of Reason in the Life of the Soul* by J. P. Moreland
- *Thinking and Acting Like a Christian: Love the Lord Your God with All Your Mind* by D. Bruce Lockerbie
- *Contours of a Worldview* by Arthur Holmes

Biblical Worldview: Behavioral Dimension

- *Every Good Endeavor: Connecting Your Work to God's Work* by Timothy Keller
- *Understanding the Culture: A Survey of Cultural Engagement* by Jeff Myers
- *Restoring All Things: God's Audacious Plan to Change the World Through Everyday People* by John Stonestreet and Warren Cole Smith
- *7 Men and the Secret of Their Greatness* by Eric Metaxas
- *7 Women and the Secret of Their Greatness* by Eric Metaxas
- *Redeeming the Routines: Bringing Theology to Life* by Robert Banks
- *Cultural Engagement: A Crash Course in Contemporary Issues* by Josh D. Chatraw and Karen Swallow Prior

Biblical Worldview in Education

- *By Design: Developing a Philosophy of Education Informed by a Christian Worldview* by Martha E. MacCullough
- *A Christian Paideia: The Habitual Vision of Greatness* by D. Bruce Lockerbie
- *Bring It to Life: Christian Education and the Transformative Power of Service-Learning* by Lynn Swaner and Roger Erdvig
- *On Christian Teaching: Practicing Faith in the Classroom* by David Smith
- *Educating for Responsible Action* by Nicholas Wolterstorff
- *Education: A Student's Guide* by Ted Newell

Science

- *The Natural Sciences: A Student's Guide* by John A. Bloom

- *Christianity and the Nature of Science: A Philosophical Investigation* by J. P. Moreland
- *Darwin's Doubt: The Explosive Origin of Animal Life and the Case for Intelligent Design* by Stephen C. Meyer
- *God's Crime Scene: A Cold Case Detective Examines Evidence for a Divinely Created Universe* by J. Warner Wallace
- *Where the Conflict Really Lies: Science, Religion, and Naturalism* by Alvin Plantinga
- *Redeeming Science: A God-Centered Approach* by Vern Poythress
- *The Soul of Science: Christian Faith and Natural Philosophy* by Nancy Pearcey and Charles Thaxton

Math

- *Redeeming Mathematics: A God-Centered Approach* by Vern Poythress
- *Truth and the Transcendent: The Origin, Nature, and Purpose of Mathematics* by Larry L. Zimmerman
- *Beyond Numbers: A Practical Guide to Teaching Math Biblically* by Katherine Loop
- *Mathematics: Is God Silent?* by James Nickel
- *Mathematics through the Eyes of Faith* by James Bradley and Russell Howell
- *Mathematics in a Postmodern Age: A Christian Perspective* by Russell Howell

Literature/English/Language Arts

- *Dismissing God: Modern Writers' Struggle Against Religion* by D. Bruce Lockerbie
- *Literature: A Student's Guide* by Louis Markos

- *Reading Between the Lines: A Christian Guide to Literature* by Gene Edward Veith
- *On Reading Well: Finding the Good Life Through Great Books* by Karen Swallow Prior
- *Literature through the Eyes of Faith* by Susan V. Gallagher and Roger Lundin
- *Media, Journalism, and Communication: A Student's Guide* by Read Mercer Shuchardt

History

- *History: A Student's Guide* by Nathan A. Finn
- *Political Thought: A Student's Guide* by Hunter Baker
- *Patterns of History: A Christian Perspective on Historical Thought* by David W. Bebbington
- *Did America Have a Christian Founding? Separating Modern Myths from Historical Truth* by Mark David Hall
- *History through the Eyes of Faith* by Ronald Wells
- *The Purpose of God's Creation* by Joseph K. Geiger
- *A History of the American People* by Paul Johnson

Fine Arts

- *Arts and Music: A Student's Guide* by Paul Munson and Joshua Farris Drake
- *Arts and the Bible* by Francis Schaeffer
- *The Liberated Imagination: Thinking Christianly about the Arts* by Leland Ryken
- *Art for God's Sake: A Call to Recover the Arts* by Philip Graham Ryken
- *Culture Care: Reconnecting with Beauty for Our Common Life* by Makoto Fujimura

- *Saving Leonardo: A Call to Resist the Secular Assault on Mind, Morals, and Meaning* by Nancy Pearcey

Athletics

- *The Christian Athlete: Honoring God in Sports* by Dwayne K. Smith
- *Christmanship: A Theology of Competition and Sport* by Greg Linville
- *A Brief Theology of Sport* by Lincoln Harvey
- *The Reason for Sports: A Christian Fanifesto* by Ted Kluck
- *In the Arena: The Promise of Sports for Christian Discipleship* by David Prince
- *The Assist: A Gospel-Centered Guide to Glorifying God through Sports* by Brian Smith

ENDNOTES

[1] For example, in a recent survey, 2,309 faculty members from forty-eight Christian colleges and universities were asked how their theological traditions impacted their teaching methods. A full 60 percent said that either they didn't know how their theological traditions influenced their teaching methods or that their teaching methods were not impacted at all by their theological traditions (Smith, 2018, p. 145).

[2] A truth claim is a statement or an unstated assumption about what a worldview purports to be true. Also, I'm assuming that if you're reading this book, we're on the same basic page relative to other key terms, such as truth, reality, knowledge, learning, and so on. For instance, I define truth as a "representation of reality that actually conforms to reality" or "a statement of the way things actually are."

[3] This is where we get the word *pedagogy*, though, as Smith points out, that word has devolved into meaning the techniques teachers use in the front of the classroom to transfer content to students.

[4] We don't have time or space to unpack these ideas here, so I'll refer you to my friend Jeff Myers's excellent works: *Understanding the Times* and his more accessible *The Secret Battle of Ideas about God*. If you really want to know about the worldviews that form the foundation for our educational system, these two are must-reads.

[5] Schools in the Christian and Dutch Reformed and Presbyterian churches in America were decades ahead of the broader Evangelical community, thanks to the work of Reformed thinkers such as James Orr, Abraham Kuyper, and Herman Dooyeweerd and institutions such as Calvin College. Unfortunately, the work of these and others who were writing on the concept of worldview before Francis Schaeffer did not gain much traction outside of the Reformed church and their institutions. For a full treatment of the migration of worldview thinking from the Reformed community to the broader Evangelical community, see David Naugle's excellent and exhaustive work, *Worldview: History of a Concept* (2002).

[6] Interestingly, postmodernism, one of the worldviews prominent in our culture, especially in the arts and entertainment, rejects the idea that a reliable organizing narrative actually exists and simultaneously insists that truth claims (accurate representations of reality) are relative and fully dependent upon the experience and perspective of individuals.

This explains our culture's rejection of the historical Christian story. It also explains how so many in our culture are fine with your truth and my truth coexisting as both equally true, in spite of the fact that they may be completely opposite representations of the way things actually are. Of course, this only works until your truth impinges upon my right to have my truth, in which case your truth is no longer true.

[7] The Gutenberg-to-Google Revolution is a concept popularized by Tom Wheeler, former chair of the Federal Communications Commission. The basic idea is that what Gutenberg's printing press did for the accessibility of knowledge in the late 1400s, the internet ("Google") has done for the modern age. The printing press revolutionized learning by allowing mass production of books, allowing ideas to travel long distances and to many people. Learning has once again been revolutionized by the internet, and ideas no longer need to travel. They are instantly accessible to anyone, anywhere, and at any time. For more on this, see Wheeler's *From Gutenberg to Google: The History of Our Future.*

8 Summit Ministries has a similar assessment for high school students at summit.org/checkup.

9 For a fascinating explanation of how intentional exposure to contrary ideas helps to inoculate individuals against those ideas and the larger world-views from which they emerge, see page 10 of *Understanding the Times* (Myers & Noebel, 2015).

10 I should also note that Summit Ministries' high school curricula takes a similar approach with students. Through their biblical worldview course, students read Darwin, Marx, Freud, Nietzsche, and numerous other non-Christian sources.

11 I'm not so sure Mr. Dewey or any other secular educationalist would agree with my definition, since I added that reflection must be tied to what one already knows to be true. As the successors of John Dewey, many if not most of today's educational leaders and practitioners are careful to avoid making statements that suggest there is truth that is true for everyone. Here is one of the nuanced ways in which teaching can be distinctive-ly Christian in nature. It unashamedly promotes the concept of absolute truth, meaning there is only one truth about any subject, concept, or idea; that truth is knowable; and that all learning is connected to the truth one already knows.

12 The faculty members in my current school have studied this book and sat under Bill's teaching. Nothing comes even close to the impact he has had on shaping the engaged learning in my school.

13 For a comprehensive treatment of service-learning in Christian schools, along with practical support in implementing it in your classroom or in a school-wide initiative, see my other work, co-authored with Dr. Lynn Swaner, published in 2018 by ACSI, *Bring It to Life: Christian Education and the Transformative Power of Service-Learning.*

[14] To aid in your ongoing seeking, pondering, and arranging of truth claims for your reservoir, the appendix of this book includes additional resources for each subject area.

[15] Dr. Mohler's example here brings up another reason to have a steady diet of this kind of input. Not only is there a benefit to hearing the truth claims that will shape your thinking, hearing a master teacher like Dr. Mohler serves as a great template for your own teaching. You can learn content *and* pedagogy.